The Great
NORTHERN
COOKBOOK

SEAN WILSON

HODDER &
STOUGHTON

First published in Great Britain in 2012 by Hodder & Stoughton
An Hachette UK company

1

Food photography © Amanda Heywood

Location photography © Transparent Television

Additional sources: p.3 © FreeSoulProduction/Shutterstock, p.4 © Anneka Sandher, p.26 © Paul Aniszewski/Shutterstock, p.40 © chris2766/Shutterstock, p.46 © albinoni/Shutterstock, p.58 © petejeff/Shutterstock, p.73 © ronfromyork/Shutterstock (centre right), p.76, p.134, p.200 © Kevin Eaves/Shutterstock, p.92 © stocker1970/Shutterstock, p.110 © Tom Curtis/Shutterstock, p.112 © Adrian Lindlay/Shutterstock, p.168 © Christian Wilkinson/Shutterstock, p.182 © Naomi Jones/Shutterstock, p.188 © George Green/Shutterstock, p.199 © tlorna/Shutterstock, p.212 © Alastair Wallace/Shutterstock.

A CIP catalogue record for this title is available from the British Library

Hardback ISBN 978 1 444 76113 9
Ebook ISBN 978 1 444 76114 6

Designed by Ashley Western www.ash.gb.com

Typeset in Eames Century Modern and Clarendon

Printed and bound by Butler Tanner & Dennis Ltd.

Hodder & Stoughton policy is to use papers that are natural, renewable and recyclable products and made from wood grown in sustainable forests. The logging and manufacturing processes are expected to conform to the environmental regulations of the country of origin.

Hodder & Stoughton Ltd
338 Euston Road
London NW1 3BH

www.hodder.co.uk

**To Callum and Maisie,
and all the cooks of tomorrow**

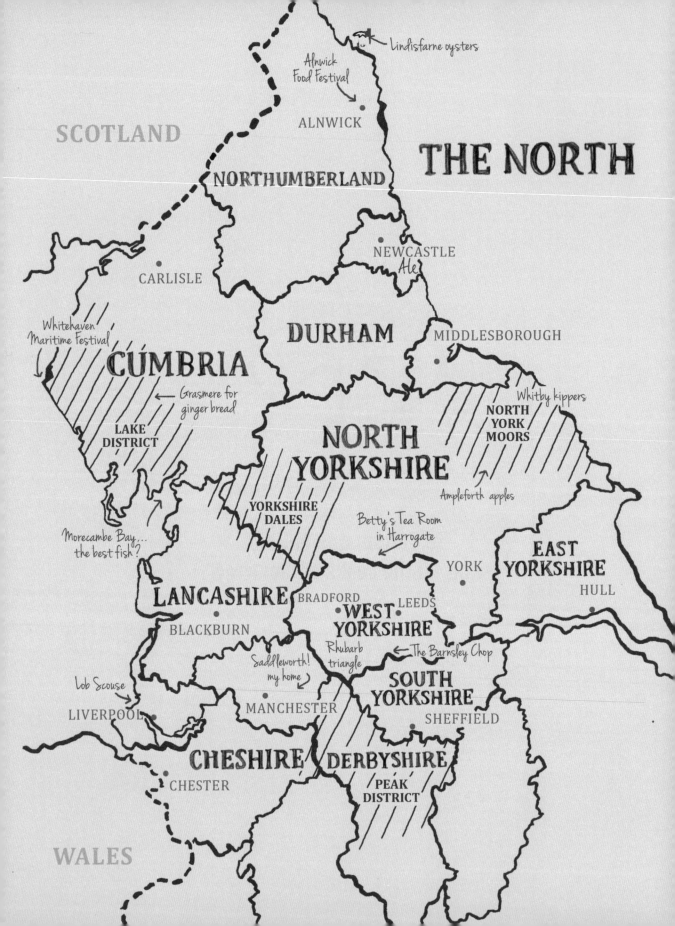

SCOTLAND

THE NORTH

Lindisfarne oysters

Alnwick
Food Festival
ALNWICK

NORTHUMBERLAND

NEWCASTLE
Ale

CARLISLE

DURHAM

MIDDLESBOROUGH

Whitehaven
Maritime Festival

CUMBRIA

Grasmere for
ginger bread

Whitby kippers

NORTH
YORK
MOORS

LAKE
DISTRICT

NORTH
YORKSHIRE

Ampleforth apples

YORKSHIRE
DALES

Betty's Tea Room
in Harrogate

YORK

EAST
YORKSHIRE

Morecambe Bay...
the best fish?

HULL

LANCASHIRE

BRADFORD   LEEDS

WEST
YORKSHIRE

BLACKBURN

Rhubarb
triangle

The Barnsley Chop

Lob Scouse

Saddleworth!
my home

SOUTH
YORKSHIRE

LIVERPOOL

MANCHESTER

SHEFFIELD

CHESHIRE

DERBYSHIRE

CHESTER

PEAK
DISTRICT

WALES

CONTENTS

INTRODUCTION

I'm a born-and-bred Northerner and have always lived in and around the northeast of Manchester, first in Ashton-under-Lyne and, for the last 20 years, in Saddleworth. When I was a kid, Ashton was a vibrant market town, with maybe a hundred stalls selling everything from groceries, fish and meat to handbags, knickers and pushbikes. At the weekends, thousands upon thousands of people descended to do their 'weekend' shop, and the market town was full to bursting with chatter and bustle. There were stalls selling faggots and savoury duck, bacons and hams of every description, plus layered sheets of honeycomb and seam (tripe) with big yellow lumps of elder (boiled cow's udder) and cowheel (yes, the heel of a cow). Further on were stalls selling oven-bottom muffins – and nothing else – as queues of folk gathered patiently, awaiting their turn to buy good produce with old-fashioned Northern integrity.

When I was eight, we moved a mile or so from Ashton-under-Lyne to a cul-de-sac where one of my biggest, life-changing decisions was made. In that cul-de-sac I decided whether I would be 'red' or 'blue' – United or City. Choosing the football team you would support for the rest of your life was big business for all Manchester kids, and it was no different for me. I became a red, through and through, and plastered my bedroom walls with newspaper clippings of my Man U hero, Lou Macari. I was a red, all right, and I combined my passion for football with making bogies and playing war in the 'big house' at the top of the road, where the main thoroughfare defined the boundaries of my childhood world.

Our grub was ordinary: chips, egg and beans, and the occasional plate pie for birthdays. *Mmm*, I can smell those pies now – cheese and onion, my personal favourite, or the equally nice alternative, meat and potato. We were tomato sauce and tomato soup kids, although oxtail soup and chips were particularly welcome after a day playing football in the park. The summer months meant salads and the only time of year when we'd actually see a raw tomato. We'd suspiciously poke around our plates, requesting identification of the ingredients, and my mum would say, 'That's cucumber, that's potato salad, and them there are radishes. Now get them down yer! They're good for you!' These early lessons in nutrition probably left some mark, but food certainly wasn't my biggest priority back then.

Fun-filled days left little time for contemplating what was on the menu, but I do remember Bonfire Nights, when I was determined to cook the perfect baked potato – wrapped carefully in foil and placed on the fire.

I got it down to a fine art. And I remember stopping dead in my tracks when I first tasted a cup of black peas with black pepper and a dash of malt vinegar. Gorgeous! It was good, honest Northern grub and, if I didn't know it then, it sparked a love affair with food that would last a lifetime.

Lessons from Grandma's kitchen

Fast forward to 1980, when I was fifteen. On Saturday mornings I could be found working on the handbag stall at the outdoor market to earn some cash. My first girlfriend worked on one of the ninety UCP Tripe stalls dotted around the Manchester markets – a tribute to a dish that all good Northerners savour. At the indoor market there was a breakfast stall that sold the best cheese on toast I've ever tasted. The owner created a blend of cheese, Worcestershire sauce and other, probably secret, ingredients, spread it on toast, grilled the lot and created the most impressive morning-hunger killers I've ever known. Of course, I later learned that these toasties were his version of Welsh rarebit, but they remain one of my earliest culinary influences.

One thing's for certain, though I was definitely not welcome in my Mum's kitchen. The only place where I could experiment with food and literally feed my early passion for the stuff was at Grandma's house in Rochdale. Here we had 'different' food: corn on the cob, crinkle-cut chips and morning porridge gleaming with golden syrup. My beloved Grandma Mona and I spent a lot of time together in her cosy kitchen and she opened up a whole new world for me. We had Bury black pudding (it was only later that she divulged the gory ingredients and, because of our special bond, it didn't matter anyway – it was lovely!) We would have Brisket Pots of lush-tasting beef with a thick gravy and vegetables, and homemade trifle with silver balls on the top. Best of all, she was a goldmine of advice that would shape my formative years, and always had a fascinating story, a hint or a titbit of information to pass on. She and my Granddad made time for us kids, introducing me to hobbies and interests, including the one that has now become my career– food. My Grandma was genuinely interesting and unique, quite unlike anyone at my own home, or anyone else's for that matter. Truth be told, apart from her we Northerners were all very similar in those days – and bloody proud of it!

A dramatic opening

With A grades in O-level Art and Drama, average grades in English and Maths, and the proud owner of a B in A-level Art, I left school in 1981 with big dreams of carving out a career in acting. My A-level Drama teacher had often remarked upon my 'great promise' and praise like this really meant something coming from a Northern teacher because as a race we're not known for false flattery. I enrolled to study at the Grange Arts Centre in Oldham, and I also joined the Oldham Theatre workshop where a hundred young men and women performed shows that ranged from original musicals through to Brecht. Before long I was hooked.

Through the theatre workshop, I was invited to audition for Granada TV in Manchester. The part? A new character on *Coronation Street* – a dream come true for any Northern lad! A week later, just before Christmas 1983, I found myself auditioning in front of *Corrie*'s director and the casting director, Judy Hayfield, and not long afterwards my agent broke the news that I'd been chosen to return in January to start work on the show. Time to grow up fast. As every good *Corrie* fan will tell you, it's the world's longest-running soap and it has pretty much a cult following. Let me tell you, I was one very proud teenager.

At the age of nineteen, I tentatively pushed opened *Coronation Street*'s green-room door, breathlessly awaiting my debut as 'Martin Platt'. I was daunted about meeting all those very famous colleagues, but I needn't have worried because straight away I was welcomed into TV's most famous Northern family. The writers and I provided Martin with a credible life and character, and I threw myself into the part, thrilling the eighteen million-strong viewers with numerous extraordinary storylines. Believe me, I was as excited as any member of the British public by the roller-coaster ride of diverse stories: a marriage with an age gap of ten years, put under strain by a babysitter with a warped infatuation; a marriage breakdown and a soulmate love affair; the pregnancy of a teenage daughter; and the struggle to keep an ever-growing family afloat on the vocational wages of a male nurse. These were just a few of the many twists and turns that Martin and I took together during trailblazing times at *Coronation Street*.

However great the *Corrie* years were though, by 2005 I knew my tenure on The Street had to end. An editorial decision had been made that Martin should embark on an under-age relationship, something that made me uncomfortable. I picked up my coat and left in September of that year, ending twenty-one years of massive fun with a fabulous on-set family. They are times I'll always remember with gratitude. But in the back of my mind, I already had an idea what I wanted to do next...

The wonderful world of food

Just after I started on *Corrie*, enigmatic chef Keith Floyd also hit our screens with his much-revered series *Floyd on Fish*, followed a couple of years later by *Floyd on France*. With this vehicle, Monsieur Floyd

managed to do for British home cooking what Henry Ford did for the motorcar: he made food chic and trendy and he stripped away the anxiety of men who wanted to cook, but were too scared to try. A self-effacing chef with a penchant for a 'slurp' of fine Burgundy, Floyd managed to bring a sense of humour into the kitchen, giving us British wannabe home chefs the oxygen boost of confidence we needed to give it a go. We suddenly felt as if we could at least *think* about cooking up a storm for our family and friends, and enjoying good food made with fine ingredients in the process. Keith Floyd made it all look *fun*!

And, wow, he was right. With a huge range of ingredients newly available in supermarkets, butchers and greengrocers, and wine becoming a staple on British menus, we could cook Keith-style. Artichokes, wild mushrooms and fresh herbs were widely stocked by the late 1980s, alongside free-range chickens, single-herd beef and even oysters. *Voilà!* I was soon cooking regional French dishes like Coq au Vin, simmered in a full bottle of Burgundy,and served to good friends with a warm baguette. I can still taste the flavours and the camaraderie today.

And so it was that I began a deeper involvement with food – not just any food, but food with integrity and taste. I *loved* being in the kitchen and started building up my beloved collection of cookery books. It was through Floyd and my cookery-book obsession that my thirty-year lesson in cooking began, and it continues to this day. I'm still hooked on new and enthralling ways to produce and prepare good food, and the techniques and science involved. I've got a real cheffy curiosity!

I am constantly grateful that I've been able to afford to indulge my insatiable interest in fine food. I've had the opportunity to visit some of the best restaurants in the UK – and Europe – many times. I've been fortunate enough to meet some top chefs, and they've given me real insight into the fascinating world of great cooking; I know what books chefs read, and which are the best French Michelin-starred restaurants. I've sampled a huge range of regional cooking, and been given amazing pointers in the yummy direction of provincial cheeses and extraordinary wines. I've also tasted (and quaffed) some damn fine plonks en route (hic!) But it was cheese that was to become an obsession.

The big cheese

In 1986, slotted in between the madness of the *Corrie* filming schedule, I took a little foray through Burgundy, where I found myself in the village of Morey-Saint-Denis, right in the heart of 'Floyd land'. I was staying in a château that was presided over by a very austere landlady. One evening

she served up a curious-looking cheese and when I asked its name, she produced an impressive Gallic tut and a roll of the eyes.

'L'Ami du Chambertin,' she said, with more than a hint of disapproval.

It was a tiny, whole cheese, about the size of a small Camembert, which had been produced for a couple to share. Its exterior was slightly aged and crinkly, and it was a pale orange colour. When I tentatively cut into it, the interior was similar to ice cream, with a fluffiness that you wouldn't normally associate with cheese. Its edges almost melted away as I reached the fudgy centre. In the end, I had to discard the knife in favour of a more appropriate spoon with which to tackle '*le fromage*' and taste this creamy, naughty-looking wheel in front of me. But first the smell: pungent and farmyard, perhaps even acidic. On a scale of one to ten for strength of 'scent', it was a good nine, or more! I took a taste and was, quite simply, transported into raptures of superlatives. *Mmmm*: creamy and unctuous, with a flavour quite unlike its smell. It was sweet and delicate and, in my humble opinion, an example of cheese-making art. It drove me straight back to my glass of Burgundy wine, which, in turn, made this robust yet velvety, powerful-smelling cheese taste even better. I was in love with a piece of cheese!

The very next morning I headed round to a local *fromager*, asking questions. It transpires that this cheese is washed in Marc de Bourgogne (a French spirit created from the by-products of wine-making). As my expert explained, 'It's a happy accident when the Marc spirit hits the milk enzymes in the high humidity of the cold cellar...'

A happy accident it most certainly was, and this single cheese was responsible for starting me on a journey that would take me from happy Floyd-style cooking to being a true lover of *real* produce that lives and breathes integrity. In 1986, we were, here in the UK, quite simply light years behind in terms of food appreciation. There may have been great, inspiring ingredients on the shelves, but not many people knew what to do with them. I remember trying to share my excitement about recent meals with *Corrie* colleagues and friends, but was always met with blank stares that implied, 'OK, moving swiftly on.' No-one understood.

I went on to taste Époisses de Bourgogne, a more famous and widely travelled Burgundy cheese that is equally pungent, but lacking the farmhouse finesse of L'Ami du Chambertin. I tiptoed with reverence into French *fromageries*, whispering to proprietors that I was on the hunt for even more delectable French provincial cheeses. I tasted the delights of Selles-sur-Cher (a French goat's cheese in an eight-centimetre-long cylinder, with a bloomy charcoal exterior and a fresh white interior with a hint of lemon) and Pouligny-Saint-Pierre (a small, tapered, pyramid-shaped chèvre with a dry, slightly crumbly interior and a herbal, nutty flavour). I was now on my own learning curve, and not Mr Floyd's. Keith had lit my fire, but I was fully capable of fanning the flames myself and it was well and truly ablaze!

Real food

Helen Worth, my dear friend and screen 'wife' during the many happy years of playing Martin Platt in *Corrie*, introduced me to Simon Hopkinson, the chef at Bibendum restaurant in London, and we spent many long hours drinking together and chatting about our mutually beloved subject: food. Simon had little respect for 'top-notch' Michelin-starred food.

'It's just not for me,' he said. 'It's lost the "real" qualities that food should *always* have.' His ethos was that food should, most importantly, be *fun*.

It was around this time I moved to Saddleworth, my next Northern home. Ah, Saddleworth, with its dry-stone walls and fields of bilberries and walking hills that stretch as far as the eye can see; its reservoirs and canal system; its mills, and its little villages and hamlets in the valleys with their pubs, butchers, bakers and post offices. It's hard to think of anywhere more idyllic, especially if you're into your Northern grub.

I spent more and more time in the local markets and in the kitchen of my new home. I toiled away making exquisite Michel Roux sweets and found

myself carefully measuring temperatures and liquid glucose, weighing minute quantities of ingredients, perfecting deliciously light meringues, spinning glimmering strands of sugar and creating fragrant, delectable almond pastes. However, Simon's words remained in the back of my mind, and they were beginning to amplify. I started casting elsewhere for inspiration. Simon's cookbooks led me to Elizabeth David and her fabulous approach to home cookery that drew on ingredients and tastes from other cultures. She travelled seemingly everywhere and introduced the Great British public (including me) to a wealth of new ideas. This was it! This was going to be *my* style of cooking! I felt at home in her books; I felt a sense of belonging.

Fresh ideas

For twenty-one years I had lived my life as a 'soap celebrity', often gazing out through that green-room window, wishing I could make something more from my life. When I made, as the tabloids coined it, my 'dramatic exit', I knew there were other horizons stretching in front of me and I was determined to explore them. I was free to spread my wings and meet the world head on.

For a couple more years I continued to work as an actor, with a little pleasing success, but something else was going on behind the scenes. My cooking was taking me to places I had never been before. I was creating my own recipes for black puddings, which I tasted and shared with my friends; I reworked raised pork pies and produced my own tangy piccalilli. I found an amazing recipe for potted beef – usually a bland, slightly beefy-tasting sludge, which I remembered from my sandwich-eating days in primary school – and was literally blown away by how divine it could taste using a different cut of beef.

I was, in fact, becoming a bit of a regular at the butchers, constantly looking for something a little out of the ordinary. Most butchers that I frequent assume the same quizzical look when I enter the shop.

'Oh, bloody hell! 'Ere 'e is. What d'ya want this time?' is often the opening gambit from butchers here up North. Yet we've now become friends, with a strong and mutual respect for and interest in each other, and a good, playful sense of fun.

It was 'Alf the butcher', as he's known round here, who gave me the meat from the lower shin of a cut of beef that made the perfect potted beef. Simmered until it begins to 'rag', seasoned with sea salt and black pepper, piled into a pudding bowl, and then packed down and weighted, it produced an irresistible meat feast, with all the qualities that real food should have. The kitchen was beginning to resemble Crippens' cellar with my homemade black puddings and experimentation with new and interesting cuts of meat, but I also baked tantalising breads with fresh yeast and made dozens of varieties of jams. I was making almond pastes and using templates to create crispy marzipan casings for lemon mousse accompanied by Kirsch-swilled cherries. I was using gelatine leaves to make ham hock terrines wrapped in cabbage leaves, and lightly vinegaring vegetables to match up the flavours. I was gleaning inspiration from the likes of Paul Heathcote, whose Michelin-starred restaurant was creating fine dining with a Northern twist: black pudding breads with scallops, and wobbly bread and butter pudding with brown bread ice cream. It was all fascinating stuff for me.

And then I got the phone call that would change things dramatically. Nigel Haworth, one of the stars of *Great British Menu* and an award-winning Lancashire chef, offered me the opportunity to work in the kitchens of Northcote Manor, a sumptuous, Michelin-starred restaurant located in the curiously named village of Langho, on the outskirts of Blackburn. Nigel was a well-known advocate of seasonal, local produce, drawn from within a fifty-kilometre radius of the restaurant, and this ethos appealed to my own thinking. I would have a chance to see if I was any good in a 'real' kitchen, working under the auspices of Nigel's chef, the wonderful Lisa Allen.

During my brief time there, I was given some incredible challenges. I boned two hundred pigeons, made Lancashire cheese ice cream and took over the production of a popular starter: a Michelin twist on egg mayonnaise. As Lisa's confidence in me grew, I progressed to dressing meals on the plates before they were presented to the guests *'en place'*, which proved to me that I could, without a doubt, make a go of this – and more! Lisa was supportive and suggested that it was a career I should consider in the future, which was high praise indeed coming from a Northerner.

Don't forget the cheese, Gromit...

The Lancashire cheese that I used to create Northcote Manor's inimitable ice cream was made by Bob Kitching from Leagram Organic Dairy in Chipping, in the beautiful Trough of Bowland. Bob, I was told, made organic Lancashire cheese by hand, and was the only organic cheesemaker in the county. That was just one reason why Nigel loved his produce so much, and the cheeses I tasted from Leagram were faultless. I made a mental note to pay a visit to Bob one day, to see how he worked.

Fast forward a week: I was asked to present a breakfast show for BBC Radio Lancashire, filling in for the enigmatic anchorman Ted Robbins. Truth be told, I'd never hosted a radio show in my life, but I was up for a challenge – and those new horizons – so I agreed. Monday morning arrived and I met with producer Alison, who patiently explained how the show would unfold. The first guest was, she announced, *Bob Kitching, a Lancashire cheesemaker*. You could have knocked me over with a feather!

'Wow!' I shouted. 'I know about Bob, and I just love cheese. I'm so looking forward to meeting him! In fact, I might ask him if I can make some cheese with him!' When I looked up from my coffee, Alison was staring at me with her mouth wide open, her eyebrows raised quizzically. 'Sean,' said she, with exaggerated patience, 'you are a "soap star". What's with all this talk about cheese?' I smiled enigmatically and headed towards the studio.

The show was a hit. I met Bob and his lovely daughter Faye, and we dissected the whole world of Lancashire cheese. I explained my growing affection for cooking, and told Bob about my adventures with French cheeses. I described how the 'science' of food really appealed to me, and

before I knew it our conversation suddenly sparked an idea: why didn't I try to make Lancashire cheese myself?

Bob gave me his card, and suggested I call him. A business making cheese – fantastic! It was obviously some sort of fate at work. I took up Bob's offer, and he showed me how to make a Lancashire crumbly cheese that set me firmly on the path I'm treading today. I went home, dragged out two large pans and some Saddleworth milk, and set to work making my own homemade cheese. With forty-four years as a cheese-lover (not to mention a little help from Bob on the phone), I was able to produce a properly pressed and waxed Lancashire crumbly to be proud of. It was all my own doing, and it felt *great*.

With Bob's guidance, I approached a dairy with its own three-hundred-strong herd of Holstein Friesian cows and asked if I could 'hire the floor' to make my cheese on a commercial basis. I'd start small, of course, but it wasn't long before my three handmade cheeses – Crumbly, Creamy and Tasty Lancashire – were in production. I was quite literally putting money where my big mouth was, but I just knew it was going to work.

So there I was, in July 2009, with only one month's production under my belt. The intake for the British Cheese Awards was upon us, and I tentatively entered my Lancashire crumbly, now named Muldoons Picnic, in the 'All Traditional Crumbly Cheeses' category. This included everything from Cheshires and Wensleydales to Caerphillys and I was sure I didn't stand a chance against such fine competition. Well, would you believe that Muldoons Picnic was judged best in category, winning a gold medal at the awards ceremony at Cardiff Castle? I simply could *not* believe it! And that, dear reader, is how my own cheesemaking company – The Saddleworth Cheese Company – was born.

Singing the blues

My crumbly success spurred me on to make a Lancashire blue, and I attended a 'soft-cheese' course at Reaseheath College in Nantwich, Cheshire. We were shown how to make an 'Ashby Blue' by Chris Ashby, the enigmatic authority on Stiltons. It was a revelation, and I was soon making and developing blue cheese at home. I had cheese in the porch, in the back room, in the kitchen and crammed into every fridge. Each had to be stored at different temperatures and humidity levels, which required constant monitoring. I toiled tirelessly for months, trying and binning so many prototypes my head was spinning. Eventually, however, I created a consistent recipe that had its origins in 'Ashby Blue' and, before that, I believe, Dovedale Blue.

With it's pure-white body, and full blue veins, my Italian-looking cheese has an amazing creaminess that is reminiscent of L'Ami du Chambertin that I tasted all those years before. With its velvety, light flavour and a pleasing, sweet nuttiness, Smelly Ha'peth was born! My range of four cheeses was now complete: Muldoons Picnic, Lancashire Crumbly; How's Yer Father, Lancashire Creamy; Mouth Almighty, Lancashire Tasty; and Smelly Ha'peth, Lancashire Blue Cheese.

Just recently, Smelly Ha'peth won a gold medal at the World Cheese Awards in the 'Any Cheese Wrapped in Foil' category, with St Agur coming second and Gorgonzola crumbly in third. Unbelievable! My French-style, handmade, cave-aged cheese just beat some of the world's finest cheese offerings. Someone pinch me, please.

Scripts, pubs and rock 'n' roll

Rev and I have known each other for donkey's years, as they say up here in the North of England. We first met way back in 1979, when I was a wee slip of a lad, at my first girlfriend's house. We soon got to chatting about show business – his love of rock 'n' roll and my new-found passion for acting. Rev had just signed his first record contract with MCA Records and I was learning the ropes at the Oldham Theatre Workshop, and after quite a few nights out, we forged a friendship away from the confines of my girlfriend's house. Fast forward on, a couple of record contracts for Rev and a handful of TV appearances for me (which culminated in my appointment to *Coronation Street*), and we made the decision to create a bachelor house *extraordinaire* in 1984. It was there that we fell for old Floydy's TV series and steamed into cooking like you wouldn't believe. Wild horses couldn't keep us away from the bookshop (or the wine shop) and as well as French cooking, we started looking locally, putting twists on Northern favourites and experimenting all over the place.

But as we threw ourselves into our careers, we ended up moving in different directions and lost touch for about ten years. Rev's achievements during that time were absolutely legendary. He followed his dream with the second-generation Icicle Works, under the very talented auspices of Ian McNabb, its founder and the songwriter of hits like 'Love Is a Wonderful Colour' and 'Birds Fly' in the 1980s. Rev is an amazing songwriter himself, and played guitar for Ian throughout those years.

It wasn't until about 2009, when I had my first taste of freedom from *Corrie* and a big dream to set up the Saddleworth Cheese Company, that I started to think of taking on a partner. I couldn't do it all on my own, and I needed a kindred spirit – someone who loved food and cooking like

I do, and had the same principles when it came to provenance. I needed someone I could trust – someone I'd be happy to spend loads of time with. I was in the pub one day, and who tapped me on the shoulder, saying, 'Alreet Cock?' but *Rev*! After a few catch-up libations, our brains were whirring and our plans were hatching. A partnership was born, and we've never looked back.

More than just cheese

Rev and I travel up and down the country spreading the gospel about our beloved Lancashire cheeses and we have taken the opportunity to visit some lovely towns and villages along the way: places that have mouth-watering ingredients of their own, such as Alnwick in Northumberland, which hosts a rapidly growing food festival each September and effortlessly brings together the sweet lamb producers of the area. We have sampled Cumbrian hogget, a lamb that is nearly matured into a sheep and whose flavours offer unique qualities that supermarkets just cannot bring; Lindisfarne oysters and mussels; and the infamous Craster crabs and lobsters. They're all famous in the region but, until our visit, we hadn't come across them. We have also fallen into the comforting arms of The Whitehaven Maritime Festival in June, where 300,000 people come along to buy all things Cumbrian. The wonderful organiser Gerard Richardson says his festival is,'Not just the tonic for Whitehaven, it's the gin and tonic!'

Through Gerard and his family we met Jean-Christophe Novelli and gasped at the superior knowledge, understanding and love of his ingredients that he so freely shares with his adoring (mostly female) audience. Jean-Christophe has a friendship with his ingredients; he knows instinctively how to match them and has the Michelin pedigree to perform anything culinary. And what's more, he's a cool, funny guy.

All these festivals are fun to go to, bringing together fabulous local ingredients and giving you the chance to meet and learn from passionate producers of fine food and top chefs of the Novelli ilk. 'Not to be sniffed at,' as my Grandma would say. There's a growing community of food lovers and cooks out there and the North has more than its fair share, with *real* food and a sense of fun that make any Northern market well worth visiting.

Good honest cooking

This book, and the TV series of the same name, have given me the exciting opportunity to bring my cooking life full circle, and to introduce you to the very best recipes from the North of England. Focussing on such a small area of the country, I have been able to delve a lot deeper into the diverse cultures, histories and traditions of the North and, of course, Northern food. The results of my travels, my many tastings, meals and experiments, are presented here, in a book that revels in its Northernness!

In this book you'll find a homely one-pot lamb hotpot that uses a classic combination of inexpensive lamb cuts and kidney, layered with potato and onion, alongside a beef stew that includes good Northern dumplings amongst its ingredients. I've fashioned an unctuous mix of traditional ox cheek with red wine and vegetables and called upon the traditions of the large Northern Jewish community to create a lush, flavourful salt beef that literally melts in your mouth. There's a timeless oxtail soup and a fresh, tasty tomato soup that will make you want to throw those tins of red stuff straight into the bin!

I've done my research and I've simplified it all to help you make your own Northern feast. I examine the world of offal in much greater detail than other books dare, and show you how to use ingredients such as tripe and lamb's hearts in delicious, nutritious, affordable meals. I've unearthed ways to create Ashton-under-Lyne's very own oven-bottom muffins; I've fished the Irish Sea and dived deep into the North Sea to gather fish and shellfish. Best of all, I've spent time with the *real* characters out there – the producers of damn fine food who are not afraid to laugh at themselves. But then we all like a good laugh up 'ere in the North and I expect to have you laughing, too.

The experts I've called on include people such as John 'Hank' Hancock, who scours the forests and grasslands of the Trough of Bowland, foraging for juicy, luscious mushrooms and berries fed by the predominantly westerly weather system that brings unpolluted rain from the Atlantic. And it's that same rain that filters through the limestone-rich land into our Northern streams and rivers to create some of the best ales – and breweries – this country has to offer. Our lush, fragrant grasses feed mostly Friesian cattle to create the finest, creamiest milk for our beloved Northern cheeses. It's a bountiful world up here in the North, and I am delighted to bring it to you with the same light-hearted sense of fun that Keith Floyd brought me back in 1984.

In the North we never take life too seriously. We have a passion for simple food, made with good, authentic ingredients and the fun that the North of England has in abundance. It's great up here, honest!

BAKING

Northern baking has an immensely rich and long tradition, and no matter what part of the North you visit, you'll not be far from a bakery or a tearoom. There's even (*shhhh*) a bit of rivalry between towns and villages, with secret recipes hoarded and local specialities feted as the best the North can offer. In fact, you'll find that very similar recipes make their way across the counties, with a few tweaks and fiddles to make them particular to specific towns and villages. For example, Eccles Cakes and Chorley Cakes are local takes on similar ingredients. Ask any local and they'll tell you that their cake is better than their neighbour's because they use treacle and not molasses, rum instead of brandy, butter over lard, sultanas instead of currants and allspice, never ginger. Most of our traditional cakes tell a story, too, with recipes that have been passed down from generation to generation, and sometimes even *stolen*!

We definitely like our stodge up here, but we also produce some of the lightest, tastiest baked goods around. There hasn't been room to include recipes for all of them here; we just have a short selection of the most famous (and, in my opinion, the best) with apologies to all the rest. Classic Northern goodies we haven't put in this book include Pikelets, a thin type of crumpet sold by the Muffin Man, Westmorland Pepper Cake, which is an unusually spicy fruitcake, and Cumberland Rum Nicky, a rich and sticky tart with dates, ginger and exotic rums that became popular in the region from Cumberland's trade with the West Indies. All Manchester school kids grew up eating Manchester cake, made with raspberry jam and custard, and with coconut and a cherry on top. Gingerbread (men and women, and nice, warm chunks) has always had a home in the North, and the famous bakery in Grasmere in the Lake District sells the best you'll find.

There's Whimberry Pie (that's what we call bilberries, roundabout Bury way); Fat Rascals topped with glacé cherries and almonds; and we'll never, ever forget our classic Ilkley Cakes from Yorkshire, with their buttery, treacly richness. There are more bakeries and bespoke cake and pastry makers in the North than anywhere else in the country, and it's easy to see why. We do the business!

If you've caught the baking bug that's been sweeping the nation, there's no better place to start than with Northern treats. There are still a few of you out there (top chefs included) who claim that you 'can't' bake, but I think that's tosh. Baking is not only one of the most immediately rewarding activities around – calming, nurturing and celebratory – but it requires you to *slooooowww* down and employ a little patience. Anyone can bake if you relax into it, I promise.

Why not start with a simple loaf of bread, which allows you to get your fingers right in there and experience the almost-instant pleasure of watching your loaf rise, prove and then bake? In fact, many good Northern meals rely upon a side of fresh bread with lashings of butter to serve. Head over to your local baker and ask for a twist of fresh yeast. That will do you for six loaves and cost you just pennies. While you are there, ask if they'll share some of their secrets. A pinch of this and a splash of that can lift a basic tart or cake to something quite sublime.

After that, go for a simple Parkin (see page 41), which is almost impossible to get wrong and lasts for simply ages! Or Singing (whistling, even!) Hinnies from Geordieland (see page 43), which make an ideal starting point for amateur bakers in need of a little Northern lift.

Top tips

Keep it light – air makes baked goods light, so fluff, fold, beat and sift to get it in there.

Always preheat your oven. If your goodies go in at the wrong temperature, they'll never bake to perfection. And invest in an oven with a light – opening and closing the door can play havoc with temperature and results.

I'm usually very relaxed about following recipes, adding a splash of this and a sprinkle of that. But when it comes to baking, you should stick to the instructions a little more closely to get the consistency just right.

ECCLES CAKES

The word 'Eccles' means 'church', and the town of Eccles takes its name from the old church (built in 1111 AD) that it grew around. From way back in the Middle Ages, a service was held to celebrate the church (known as an Eccles wake), followed by a fair where Eccles Cakes were sold. In 1650, these fragrant little cakes (and the wakes) were banned by the Puritan Oliver Cromwell because of 'pagan connections'. Luckily it wasn't long before they were back on the menu, and by 1793 a man called James Birch made them popular once again, selling them in his Eccles Cakes Shop (described by the English novelist Arnold Bennett as 'the most romantic shop in the world'). By 1818, Eccles Cakes had become so popular that they were being exported to America and the West Indies, as well as being sold at markets and fairs around the country.

Today, there is no longer any sign of the original shop and Eccles itself has been swallowed to become part of Salford in Manchester. Lancashire Eccles cakes are still made commercially, each cake containing lots of lovely butter, Vostizza currants and Demerara sugar. The Edmonds family in Adwick, Manchester,have a business that makes a whopping 750,000 cakes every week. That's some demand!

Eccles Cakes are a delight that deserve to be recognised countrywide, rather than solely within Lancashire, but truth be told the pale imitations seen elsewhere in the country have a lot of living up to do. Eccles Cake doesn't yet have 'protected geographical indication' status, so it can be manufactured anywhere else and still labelled as the real thing. Choose carefully or, better still, make your own!

The Eccles Cake is cousin to the Chorley cake, which uses the same filling but encases it in an unsweetened shortcrust pasty (rather than flaky). It doesn't have the crunchy, caramelised caster-sugar topping either, relying on a smear of fresh butter on top instead. The Garibaldi biscuit is another Eccles Cake relative, but it's a drier biscuit rather than a lovely moist cake. All go down beautifully with a cuppa Northern brew and some quality Lancashire cheese, of course!

One of the finest examples of sweet Lancastrian delicacies, the Eccles Cake is a delight that deserves to be recognised countrywide.

ECCLES CAKES

Mmmm, flaky pastry filled with small currants (dead flies), mixed with orange zest, sugar and a touch of cinnamon or nutmeg; its top slit three times to allow steam to escape. This is the quintessential Eccles Cake, which has been a favourite Northern treat for hundreds of years. As well as 'Dead Fly Pie', Eccles Cake has also been nicknamed 'Squashed Fly Cake', 'Fly Cake', 'Fly Pie' and 'Fly's Graveyard'. In our view, these divine cakes way outclass the scone and jam as an accompaniment to afternoon tea, flies or not! Serve with Lancashire cheese, of course.

MAKES 12 CAKES

100g unsalted butter

300g Demerara sugar

500g small currants
(go for Vostizza if you can
find them)

1 tsp ground cinnamon

½ tsp nutmeg

Zest of 1 orange

2 x 500g ready-made puff
pastry (made with butter,
if possible)

Plain flour, for dusting

30ml full-fat milk, for
brushing

50g melted butter, for brushing

25g caster sugar

Hand-crafted Lancashire
crumbly cheese, to
accompany (optional)

Preheat the oven to 220°C/425°F/Gas mark 7.

First, melt the butter in a small pan, taking care not to burn it.

Then, in a large bowl, mix together the melted butter, the Demerara sugar, currants, cinnamon, nutmeg and orange zest.

Roll out the puff pastry onto a lightly floured work surface to about 3mm thick (so quite thin really). Cut 12–15cm discs from the pastry using a cookie cutter or an upturned bowl.

Place a good tablespoon of the filling onto the centre of each disc, and then brush the edges of the discs with a little cold water. Next, use your fingertips to draw the edges over the filling to meet in the middle, scrunching them together to seal (this will be the underside, so don't worry about presentation at this point).

Turn over your cakes and flatten your scrunched underside by pressing down with the flat of your hand. They should be discs about 10cm across and about 1–2cm thick, depending on the amount of filling. Neaten the edges with the flat of a knife.

Cut three slits in the middle of the tops, then brush the tops with a mixture of milk and melted butter. Finally, dip in caster sugar to coat the tops.

Transfer to a greased baking tray and bake for 10–12 minutes until golden brown.

To serve, place two warm Eccles cakes on the centre of a nice white plate with a chunk of your favourite crumbly Lancashire cheese on the side.

YORKSHIRE CURD TART

Visit *any* Yorkshire bakery and you'll find a proud display of glorious Yorkshire Curd Tarts. As you know, Yorkshire folk are very proud of all things Yorkshire, and this is a particularly justifiable case! This very proud Lancastrian has whipped 'over th'ill' and stands proudly with my Yorkshire compatriots as I present to you this very, very fine example of their traditional treat. Enjoy!

For the pastry

115g unsalted butter, diced

225g plain flour

1 free-range egg yolk

For the filling

A large pinch of ground allspice (crucial!)

90g caster sugar

3 free-range eggs, beaten

Zest and juice of 1 lemon

40g unsalted butter, melted

450g curd cheese (cottage or mascarpone will suffice)

75g good-quality sultanas

Cream, to serve

Preheat the oven to 190°C/375°F/Gas mark 5.

In a large bowl, make the pastry by rubbing the butter into the flour with your fingertips until it resembles fine breadcrumbs. Stir in the egg yolk and add a little cold water to bind. Turn the dough out onto a lightly floured surface and knead lightly. Form into a ball and then roll it out thinly. Line a 20cm fluted loose-bottomed tart tin and refrigerate for 15 minutes.

While the pastry is chilling, mix together the allspice with the sugar, and then stir in the eggs, lemon zest and juice, melted butter, cheese and sultanas. Pour into the chilled pastry case and bake for 40 minutes, or until the pastry is cooked and the filling is slightly set and golden brown.

Serve still slightly warm, cut into wedges, with a side of cream.

Lip-smackingly good!

CUSTARD TART

There isn't a baker in the North who doesn't think that his or her Custard Tart is the best in town, and most pride themselves on a good 'wobble' of custard. And that, my friends, is the key: without said 'wobble', a Custard Tart is, quite simply, substandard. In my view, only bona fide bakers can produce the same thing – supermarket versions are just plain imposters! Here is my recipe for custard par excellence, created with fresh, good ingredients that are treated with respect and cooked properly.

SERVES 4

For the sweet shortcrust pastry

250g plain flour

50g icing sugar

A pinch of salt

125g unsalted butter, softened

1 free-range egg yolk

1 tsp lemon juice

3 tbsp very cold water

For the custard

3 medium free-range eggs

40g caster sugar

½ tsp cornflour

300ml full-fat milk

1 vanilla pod, sliced in half and seeds removed

Freshly grated nutmeg

To make the pastry, sift the flour, icing sugar and salt into your favourite mixing bowl. Add the butter, then rub between your fingers until you have a fine 'breadcrumb' consistency. Add the egg yolk and lemon juice and begin to gather in your dough, adding the water as required to create a satin finish. It shouldn't be too dry. Roll into a ball, cover with cling film and refrigerate for 30 minutes.

To make the custard, in a medium-sized bowl, beat the eggs and whisk in the sugar and cornflour. Continue beating until the sugar dissolves.

In a small saucepan, heat the milk with your vanilla pod and bring to the boil. Remove from the heat and slowly pour over the egg mixture, whisking continuously.

To assemble, preheat your oven to 150°C/300°F/Gas mark 2.

Next, roll out your chilled pastry on a lightly floured surface and line a greased 20cm loose-bottomed tart tin. Blind bake the pastry for 25 minutes, with some uncooked rice or baking beans on top. Cool before pouring your custard into the pastry shell you have created, and sprinkle with nutmeg.

Carefully place in the oven and bake for 30 minutes until set (give it a little wobble to check). Cool and remove from your tin to serve at room temperature.

American or English muffins won't do for us in the North ... No, it has to be a blackened Oven-Bottom Muffin, complete with hole in the centre.

MUFFINS

Muffins can be sweet or savoury, chocolatey or fruity. The American kind rises during cooking and is similar to a cupcake, while the classic English one is flat and smooth on one side, but pockmarked with craters on the other to allow as much oozing melted butter to soak in as possible. But in Lancashire we have our very own type of muffin, made in the bottom of the oven while we're cooking something else (hence the name).

In Ashton-under-Lyne market, where I first sampled the delights of the Oven-Bottom Muffin, they are known as 'backstones' because they are baked on a stone from a quarry in Saddleworth, which sits in the oven bottom and retains the heat. This gives the muffins a blackened appearance – although they're not actually burnt. They have holes in the middle, traditionally made with a knitting needle, but I tend to use my thumb. You can serve them however you like, but I have mine with a nice chunk of cheese and some homemade Piccalilli (see page 204).

Over in the Northeast, they also have a type of bread with a dip in the middle, but theirs are known as 'stotties' and they're really nothing like ours. A stottie is a round, flat loaf with a dent in the middle that the baker makes with his thumb. They tend to be quite heavy and doughy, but they're very popular, so do give them a try if you're in the region.

In the Manchester area, you may come across something called a 'barm cake', which is essentially a large bap. All of them are great for your lunchtime sarnie on the run, but I prefer our Oven-Bottom Muffins because they're light as a feather and *smooooth* to eat.

You'll find variations on all our Northern breads, and the health brigade have now introduced wholegrain varieties, of course, but you can't beat my recipe for Oven-Bottom Muffins on page 38. The great thing about doing your own baking is that your house is filled with the fantastic aroma of warm bread. Kneading dough is incredibly therapeutic and can be a great way to introduce the kids to cooking, bringing all their experience of play dough to the table. Best of all, you can grab your muffins freshly baked and piping hot from the oven. Just wait long enough so they don't completely take the mouth off you, tear off a chunk then slap on your favourite butter and tuck in. Perfect!

OVEN-BOTTOM MUFFINS

This is the definitive recipe for these amazing 'real' muffins, which beat any other American or English imposter on the planet. Over 40 million Oven-Bottom Muffins are produced each year, and once you've tried one, you'll definitely know why! Serve warm with cheese, jam, cold meat, salad – whatever takes your fancy. Anything goes.

MAKES 6–8 MUFFINS

400g strong white flour

½ tsp fine sea salt

1 tsp caster sugar

1 sachet (7g) instant dried yeast

1 tbsp salted butter, softened to room temperature

2 tsp sunflower oil

90ml full-fat milk

180ml warm water

In a large bowl, stir together the flour, salt and sugar. Add the yeast and then blend again. Don't be tempted to use a mixer – this is one recipe that must be blended by hand. Mix in the butter and oil and rub with your fingertips for a minute or two until the ingredients are nice and crumbly. Place the milk and warm water together in a measuring jug and then pour around the rim of the bowl to distribute the liquid evenly. Continue to stir by hand so that the liquid 'picks up' the dry ingredients, and then work the ingredients together for about 5 minutes to create a lovely dough. Press down lightly and cover the bowl (not the dough) with cling film. Leave in a warm place for about 60 minutes.

When the dough has doubled in size, turn it out on a floured surface and form into a long 'breadstick', then divide into six or eight pieces. Roll each piece into a ball with your hand until cool and slightly sticky. Press down on the muffins with a floured bread board to make them smooth, flat and roughly 2.5cm thick. Place on a greased baking tray and leave in a warm place for a further 30 minutes.

Preheat your oven to 200°C/400°F/Gas mark 6.

Using the floured bread board, press down again on each muffin until it is about 1cm thick. Make a big, at least thumb-sized, hole in the centre with your finger. Turn the muffins over and bake for 6 minutes. Then turn the muffins over again, return to the oven and cook for a further 5 minutes.

Cool on a wire rack and Bob's your Auntie Fanny!

MALT LOAF

Malt Loaf is a requisite of the Northern bread bin. Many a child has rushed in from school after an afternoon of PE and devoured buttered slices of this incredible loaf. Sticky, sticky, sticky! I have researched the recipe at length and put together this lovely, sticky, apricoty, malty Great Northern loaf. Enjoy! This recipe makes two small loaves because they're so good one will never be enough, but halve the ingredients if you only want one.

MAKES 2 SMALL LOAVES

Sunflower oil, for greasing

150ml hot black tea
(Yorkshire tea of course!)

175g malt extract, plus extra
for glazing

85g dark muscovado sugar

100g soft dried apricots

200g mixed dried fruits
(sultanas, raisins)

2 large free-range eggs, beaten

250g plain flour

1 tsp baking powder

1 tsp mixed spice

½ tsp bicarbonate of soda

Preheat the oven to 150°C/300°F/Gas mark 2.

Grease two loaf tins, then line the base and both ends with strips of baking parchment.

Pour the hot tea into a large mixing bowl with the malt, sugar, dried apricots and mixed dried fruit. Stir well and then add the eggs. Tip in the flour, then quickly stir in the baking powder, mixed spice and bicarbonate of soda and pour into the prepared tins. Bake for 50 minutes, until firm and well risen.

Remove from the oven and, while the loaves are still warm, brush with a little more malt to glaze. Leave to cool before removing from the tins. One of the great things about this loaf is that it gets stickier over time. If you can bear it, wrap it up and put it to one side for 2 to 5 days and then enjoy sliced and buttered.

PARKIN

Treacly, sticky, sickly sweet, gooey and most of all *gorgeous*, Parkin is a traditional Northern cake that is believed to hail from Yorkshire. Where I come from, Bonfire Night would not be complete without Parkin. All the mothers in our area would turn up with trays of the stuff and there was probably enough there to last us until Christmas. And that's no bad thing. Some Parkin connoisseurs insist upon eating it 'aged' because it gets stickier after a few days.

SERVES 4

200g golden syrup

200g black treacle

110g unsalted butter, softened to room temperature

110g soft dark brown sugar, such as muscovado

225g medium oatmeal

110g self-raising flour

3 tsp ground ginger

½ tsp nutmeg

A pinch of salt

1 large free-range egg, beaten

1 tbsp full-fat milk

Preheat the oven to 140°C/275°F/Gas mark 1.

Put your syrup, treacle, butter and sugar in a heavy-based saucepan over a medium heat, and stir until the butter and sugar have melted. Mix the dry ingredients in a mixing bowl, then add them to the saucepan and mix thoroughly until completely amalgamated. Add the beaten egg a few spoonfuls at a time and then add the milk, stirring continuously.

Line a 20cm square cake tin with greaseproof paper. Pour in your mixture and bake on the centre shelf of your oven for 75 minutes. Don't all grab at once – allow the Parkin to cool in the tin for at least 30 minutes or you'll burn your fingers and your mouth.

GOOSNARGH CAKE

Goosnargh Cake was traditionally sold at Easter and Whitsun and eaten with ale. Biscuits with a pint – that's the way forward. The original recipe has been passed around this Lancashire village for decades now, and is a highly guarded secret. This is my version (*left*).

MAKES 6–8 CAKES

1 tsp caraway seeds
250g plain flour
A pinch of salt
175g best unsalted butter, softened to room temperature
3 tbsp caster sugar

Preheat the oven to 180°C/350°F/Gas mark 4.

In a non-stick frying pan, lightly toast the caraway seeds.

Mix together the flour, salt and caraway seeds, then add the butter. Use a knife to cut through the butter and flour mix until it's crumbly and evenly mixed. Knead to a smooth dough, roll out to about 5mm thick and cut the dough into small circles using a biscuit cutter. Sprinkle with caster sugar. Place on non-stick paper and chill for an hour. Bake in the oven for 30 minutes until firm, but not browned.

SINGIN' HINNY

A 'hinny' is a large, round cake from Northumberland made from a scone mixture that is baked on a griddle, where it 'sings' and fizzes as it cooks. In parts of Northumberland they are also known as 'small coal fizzers', since they are cooked over a coal fire (it's the bicarbonate that causes the fizzing).

MAKES 4 CAKES

170g plain flour
25g ground rice
A pinch of sea salt
25g caster sugar
1 heaped tsp bicarbonate of soda
25 currants
25g best unsalted butter or lard, softened to room temperature
A little milk

Sift the dry ingredients into a mixing bowl, stir in the currants and then rub in the lard or butter with your fingers. It's fine for the mixture to be quite coarse. Mix with enough milk to make a soft, but not sticky dough. If your dough becomes too wet, simply add a little more flour.

On a floured surface, lightly roll your dough to about 1cm thick. Neatly cut a circle about 15–20cm across from the dough, and then cut your circle into quarters. Heat a hot griddle, cast-iron pan or any non-stick pan and cook your four cakes until they 'sing' – about 10 minutes on each side. Your cakes are ready when they are nicely browned on both sides and have risen slightly.

Serve hot, split and buttered.

THE NORTHERN GENTLEMAN'S AFTERNOON TEA

Over the past few years, afternoon tea has become the big thing. I see the appeal of all those dainty finger sandwiches and delicate cupcakes, stacked up on a pretty cake stand, but in all honesty you're never going to get me making cupcakes. This is my suggestion for a more robust afternoon tea that the discerning Northern gentleman will enjoy.

Potted Shrimps and toast (see page 104)

Potted Herb Cheese with roast beef on sourdough bread

Half a Pint O' Prawns with Cheat's Garlic Mayonnaise

Goosnargh Cake (see page 43)

Half an ale or a bullshot (see page 215)

Yorkshire tea

Serve as a spread on old crockery

POTTED HERB CHEESE

SERVES 3

60g Cheddar cheese

60g Lancashire crumbly cheese

50g best unsalted butter

1 tbsp chopped fresh chives

1 tbsp chopped fresh chervil (or parsley if you can't get chervil)

1 tbsp Madeira or dry sherry

A pinch of freshly ground black pepper

A pinch of good-quality sea salt

Sourdough (or any country) bread, to serve

Grate the cheeses and put with the butter into a food processor. Blend until smooth. Add the herbs and Madeira and season with the ground black pepper and sea salt. Spoon the herby cheese into individual ramekins and serve with sourdough bread or, even better, thinly sliced roast beef on sourdough bread.

HALF A PINT O' PRAWNS WITH CHEAT'S GARLIC MAYONNAISE

SERVES 1

1 garlic clove

Splash of olive oil

2 pinches of good-quality sea salt

2 dollops of good-quality supermarket mayonnaise

1 tbsp fresh parsley, finely chopped

½ pint glass of fresh cooked prawns

On a chopping board, chop the garlic as small as possible. Add a tiny splash of olive oil and the sea salt. Then, with a kitchen knife, work the oil, salt and garlic together, mashing them into a paste. Add the paste to the mayonnaise and stir the parsley into the mixture. Serve with a half pint glass full of good fresh cooked prawns.

CHEESE

B lessed are the cheesemakers!' says a spectator in Monty Python's *Life of Brian*, after mishearing a sermon on peace, love and tolerance. Hey, we say! He's got it right! Way up here in the North we have a myriad of unbelievable cheeses, with a big fat vat full of history and tradition. Northern cheeses win oodles of awards, and up here we revere cheesemakers (which may be one of the reasons why I became one!)

So we know that the Jervaulx monks of Northern France brought their cheesemaking know-how to Wensleydale in the Yorkshire Dales after the Norman Conquest in the eleventh century. They made a cheese called 'cover bridge cheese', originally from sheep's milk and then cows', which eventually became the Wensleydale we know and love today. When Henry VIII ordered the Dissolution of the Monasteries and made it a tricky time to be a monk, they managed to pass their secrets to local farmers, who continue to make this crumbly, moist cheese to this day. Look out for Wensleydale and Jervaulx Blue!

Lancashire cheeses go back to the thirteenth century, when the art of making multi-curd cheese developed. At the end of the day, farmers' wives would make a curd from any milk that was left over. It wasn't usually enough to make a whole cheese, but the next day they'd add a little more fresh curd, and so on, until a cheese was formed. In the 1880s, a farmer called Joseph Gornal was hired by Lancashire council to standardise cheese production across the region. In his wisdom, he decided that Lancashire cheese was best made with two-day curd, and so Lancashire Creamy and Lancashire Tasty were created, with recipes that are still used to this day and Lancashire remains the only county to use 'multi-curd' cheesemaking. Creamy cheese is matured for between four and twelve weeks, while anything matured for longer is classified as Tasty. Tasty Lancashire can officially be aged for up to twenty-four months.

Crumbly Lancashire is a more recent addition to the Lancashire cheese family, and it's probably the one that's best known outside the region. It was developed some forty years ago, when farmers decided they needed a cheese that could compete with Cheshire, Wensleydale and Caerphilly – and one they could get into the shops quickly! It's made with only one day's milking, and in a similar way to Cheshire cheese. After this, Lancashire Blue made an appearance, giving Lancashire four cheeses – the only county that has that many!

We've got dozens of cheeses in the North, made from all kinds of ingredients. There are goat's and ewe's cheeses (such as Tovey, Crofton and Cumbrian Allerdale), pasteurised and unpasteurised cheeses, smoked cheeses, cheeses with raisins, currants, spices, herbs and even vegetables. Some of our cheeses are our own take on classics made by other counties: for example, Goosnargh Gold is a Double Gloucester with a rich, buttery taste that we think is far superior to its Southern counterpart. Cumbrian brie is soft and silky smooth and the award-winning Bright Blessed Crest is a sheep's milk brie to die for. And my own Saddleworth Cheese Company in Lancashire...we could go on forever!

Newer cheeses are hitting the headlines, awards ceremonies and shelves up here in the North, too. At Doddington Dairy, in Wooler, Northumbria, the Maxwell family make a semi-hard cheese that's like Dutch Gouda in taste and texture. It uses unpasteurised milk and animal rennet, and they say its salty, slightly spicy flavour is due to the farm being near the North Sea coast. It's covered in a beetroot-red wax from Holland, meaning it's easy to spot in your local deli.

The Lake District Cheese Company is a twenty-first-century addition to Northern cheese production, making a mature cheddar from the milk of 350 different Cumbrian milk producers. And if you're a cheese connoisseur, be sure to try Ribblesdale goat's milk cheese made high up in the Pennines, Shepherds Purse cheeses made at a family farm near Thirsk and Suzanne Stirk's King Richard III Wensleydale.

Suffice to say that the North has many more cheesemakers than we can chuck a stick at, creating internationally famous, award-winning cheeses on a regular basis. These Great Northern cheeses have one thing in common: a particularly special creaminess. Our cows (and goats and sheep) feed on grass that's fresh, green and unpolluted, and their milk is the amazing starting point for cheesemakers like us!

Many of my recipes use traditional favourites and we urge you to try them. Search them out at the hundreds of dedicated food markets throughout the North or look for them on the internet. We've given links to a few of the best on page 218. Choosing good-quality ingredients can make a simple recipe something truly special. Northern cheese breathes life into traditional Northern fare and those cheesemakers – well, we are truly blessed!

BOILED ONIONS WITH POACHED EGG & LANCASHIRE CHEESE

I simply could not leave this curious Lancashire dish out of *The Great Northern Cookbook*. Simon Hopkinson, who hails from Bury in Lancashire, printed an original version of this recipe in his excellent book *The Vegetarian Option*, where you'll find a host of parochial dishes like this one. It's incredibly simple to arrange and cook, but it is (as Simon also assures us) absolutely 'astonishing'. The flavours take me right back home, and make me proud to be Lancastrian.

SERVES 4

500g white onions, peeled and thickly sliced

350ml water

50g salted butter

½ tsp ground white pepper

2 tsp sea salt

1 bay leaf

Splash of malt vinegar

250g Lancashire crumbly cheese

4 large free-range eggs

2 tbsp finely chopped fresh parsley

Place the onions into a pan with the water, butter, pepper, salt and bay leaf. Bring to the boil, and then reduce the heat. Cover and simmer for about 30 minutes, or until the onions are nice and soft.

Next, preheat the grill to hot. Fill a pan of water for the poached eggs, adding a splash of vinegar, and bring to a simmer. Add your eggs and poach for roughly 3 minutes – 4 if your eggs are straight from the fridge.

While your eggs are poaching, stir the onions well and divide among four ovenproof shallow dishes (about soup-bowl size). Sprinkle with the cheese and place under the grill until it is just melted, but not brown. Remove and top each dish with a poached egg. Sprinkle with parsley and serve immediately.

WELSH RAREBIT

Back when I was a kid selling handbags on a market stall on Saturdays,
I always looked forward to the moment after setting up the stall
when I was sent to the indoor market for 'cheese toasties', the most
magnificent combination of cheese, Worcestershire sauce and some other
unidentifiable ingredients, grilled to blistering perfection. It wasn't till later
that I found out that these toasties were, in fact, Welsh Rarebit. They were
simply the best!

SERVES 4

15g butter

1 tsp flour

50ml milk

1 tbsp Dijon mustard

225g Lancashire tasty cheese
(Mouth Almighty is perfect!)

60ml Guinness

Freshly ground black pepper,
to taste

1 tsp Worcestershire sauce

1 medium free-range egg,
beaten

4 slices of bread

In a saucepan, melt the butter and stir in the flour over a low
heat to form a roux. Cook the roux through to remove any
floury taste, keeping an eye on it all the time so it doesn't
become too paste like. Add the milk a drop at a time, stirring
vigorously, until the roux comes away from the side of the pan
and you're left with a creamy white sauce.

Stir in the mustard, cheese, Guinness and pepper until well
combined and then turn up the heat and let the mixture come
to a boil (think lava and volcanoes). Remove the pan from the
heat, add the Worcestershire sauce and then quickly whisk in
the egg so that it does not cook before it is combined (the egg
does cook as basically you're making a thick savoury custard,
but you don't want to boil it as it will curdle). Allow to cool.

Toast the bread on one side and then daub the topping over the
untoasted side with a palette knife. Grill under a hot grill until
intuition and aroma tells you that it's done – you'll know!

LANCASHIRE CHEESE SOUFFLÉS

I have travelled the length and breadth of the country demonstrating this lovely Northern soufflé. I try to convey to the audience that making soufflés is all about confidence – and using the right equipment. You will need proper individual soufflé ramekins with high sides, and then hopefully both you and the soufflés will rise to the occasion.

SERVES 4

50g unsalted butter, plus extra for greasing

1 onion, peeled and finely chopped

1 cob of sweetcorn

50g plain flour

350ml full-fat milk

½ to 1 tsp English mustard

150g Lancashire crumbly cheese

6 medium free-range eggs, separated

1 pickled walnut, cut into 4 slices

Salt and freshly ground black pepper, to taste

Preheat the oven to 180°C/350°F/Gas mark 4.

Melt half the butter in a heavy-based pan over a medium heat. Add the onion and cook, stirring frequently, until it is translucent. Cut the kernels from the sweetcorn and add to the onion. Sauté until the corn is partly browned and takes on a nutty smell.

In a separate pan, melt the rest of your butter and sift the flour into it. Stir briskly to get a nice roux and cook for 2 minutes. Warm the milk, then whisk it into the roux to create a smooth white sauce. Add the corn and onion to the sauce along with the mustard, some salt and pepper, cheese and four of the egg yolks. Mix thoroughly and turn off the heat.

Now, whisk all six egg whites until they are stiff enough to hold their shape (soft peaks, we chefs call it). Beat about a third of the beaten egg whites into your sauce and cheese mixture, then gently fold in the remainder of the whites. You need to keep the air in it rather than flattening it down.

Lightly butter four soufflé ramekins and half-fill with the mixture. Place a slice of pickled walnut on top of each, then fill with the remainder of the mixture. To neaten it up, put your thumb on the inside and your fingers outside the ramekin and turn it around so that you get a smooth edge on the soufflé. Put the ramekins in a roasting tin and then pour enough boiling water around them to come about halfway up the ramekins. Bake for 20 minutes.

As soon as they're ready, place each ramekin on a white plate and eat the soufflé with a teaspoon.

BLUE CHEESE ON PUFF PASTRY WITH ROCKET & TOMATOES

In the summertime, when the weather is fine, there's nothing quite like some cheese and wine! The shops are full to bursting with lush ripe tomatoes and fragrant fresh herbs. Add one to the other and enjoy with a glass of French wine for a Provençal vibe. This is a great favourite with vegetarians.

SERVES 4

12 large ripe tomatoes, halved (I like to use a mixture of types)

Olive oil, for drizzling

1 sprig of fresh rosemary, leaves removed and finely chopped

1 sprig of fresh thyme, leaves removed and finely chopped

1 small onion, peeled and finely chopped

1 garlic clove, peeled and finely chopped

A large handful of rocket

500g puff pastry (shop bought is fine)

140g Smelly Ha'peth or your own favourite blue cheese

Freshly grated Parmesan cheese

Preheat the oven to 180°C/350°F/Gas mark 4.

Place your tomatoes in a deep roasting tray. Liberally drizzle with olive oil and sprinkle with the chopped rosemary and thyme leaves. Place the roasting tray in the centre of the oven and turn it down to its lowest heat. Leave for at least 60 minutes. This process brings out the sweet richness of your ripe tomatoes.

Next, add a little olive oil to your favourite frying pan and sweat the onion and garlic until they are translucent, but not coloured. Add half of the rocket, remove from the heat and set to one side.

On a floured surface, roll out your puff pastry to form a large rectangle (about 40 x 25cm). Take a fork and prick the surface of the pastry, leaving a 5cm margin around the sides. Place on a greased baking tray and bake for 10 minutes at 180°C/350°F/Gas mark 4 until the sides have risen, but it is not coloured. This 'blind bakes' your pastry, but also allows the sides to rise slightly.

Remove your pastry from the oven and spread your garlic, onion and wilted rocket mixture over the pricked surface (not the margins). Arrange your tomatoes over the top as beautifully as you can (cheffy stuff required here!) and sprinkle with creamy blue cheese.

Return to the oven and bake for 8–10 minutes until golden brown. Remove from the oven and sprinkle with the remaining rocket and some freshly grated Parmesan cheese. Place on a bread board and serve whole on your dinner table with your favourite dressed salad.

LANCASHIRE CHEESE ICE CREAM

I was first introduced to the concept of Lancashire Cheese Ice Cream when I worked briefly at Northcote Manor in Langho, Blackburn, where Nigel Haworth was then head chef. I was asked to make it, which, of course, gave me the perfect excuse to try it – and I wasn't disappointed. When I started making my own Lancashire cheeses, I decided to give it a go myself and came up with my own version of this modern classic.

SERVES 4

420ml double cream

420ml full-fat milk

10 free-range egg yolks

150g caster sugar

150g mascarpone cheese

150g ricotta cheese

150g Lancashire cheese, grated

In a heavy-bottomed pan, bring the double cream and milk to the boil. Remove from the heat and set to one side. In a large bowl, whisk together the egg yolks and the sugar for about 2 minutes until straw-coloured. Pour in half the warm cream and milk mixture and whisk vigorously to combine. Slowly add the remaining cream and milk, whisking constantly, until smooth.

Pour into another heavy-bottomed pan and cook over low heat until the mixture is slightly thicker. This may take about 8–10 minutes. Pour into a liquidiser, add the three cheeses and liquidise on a low setting for 1 minute. Allow to cool.

Churn the ice cream in an ice-cream machine, according to manufacturer's instructions, and then transfer to a freezer-proof container and into the freezer until required. Alternatively, if you don't have an ice-cream maker, you can place it in a plastic container in the freezer, but you will have to churn it up every 20 minutes with a wooden spoon until it is set. Although it's delicious on its own, the very best way to serve this ice cream is with Apple Crumble (see page 190) or Lancashire Cheese & Apple Pie (see page 191). *Yum!*

SOUPS

We're hardy folk up here in the North. Us gents will sit through a footie match in a vest in the middle of winter, and our ladies think nothing of heading out to the clubs with bare legs and miniskirts in the snow. But there is nothing, and we mean *nothing*, more Northern than a steaming hot bowl of soup. It warms the heart and the cockles, and it keeps us going in all weather and with very little outlay. We like our grub hot, thick and filling, and we like to stretch our pennies as far as they'll go. Truth be told, we're grafters in the North, and we like big families. Soup provides a nourishing meal for a brood of hungry children, using tired, humble vegetables and leftover bones. It keeps us going when we're broke and it comforts us when we ail. Best of all, it encourages us to slow down a little…to linger over the dinner table and spend time with loved ones.

Soups can be made with leftovers and eked out over days, with an extra handful of this and that. There is literally no waste with soup, and that appeals to us Northerners' thrifty nature (as does the fact that the main ingredient of *any* soup is water). We use fresh local and seasonal produce, and no Northern kitchen is complete without a few tubs of pulses, beans and grains to turn a simple soup into a hearty meal. We add cream and good Northern cheeses to keep out the cold, and flake in fish, shellfish, inexpensive cuts of meat, chicken and even offal to bulk it all out. And we use our fish, poultry and meat bones to create delicious stocks, so every meal gets an extra outing – as soup! It goes without saying that you don't need to be a Michelin-starred chef to create a decent soup, and you can taste and taste to your heart's content as it simmers away on the stove. Even better, you can pop anything and everything into your slow cooker, cover it with loads of water or stock, and leave it to do the business while you're out and about. Instant meal, Northern-style!

In the winter, nothing is better than a Lancashire Pea & Ham Soup (see page 64), so thick your spoon rests happily upright for the next big mouthful. Roasted Tomato Soup (see page 67) is gloriously rich and hot, with the addition of cream in the colder months. Without the cream and served slightly chilled, it provides a more delicate, cooling experience when it's sweltering outside. I've even snuck in a few dishes that didn't start out here, but have become Northern family favourites. Cullen Skink (originally from Scotland, but adopted by us long ago) springs to mind (see page 70).

Northern cooks have also adopted a wide range of culinary tips from our long-established immigrant populations, with divine chicken soups and dumplings from the Jewish community, rich beety borschts from our

Eastern European compatriots, winter-warming spices that traditionally fire up Asian dishes (not to mention the now ubiquitous lentil), and a handful of the most excellent pasta and noodles, as well as a wide variety of beans, thanks to our friends from Italy.

I've always got a stock of good English root vegetables in the cellar or the bottom drawer of the fridge, and carrots, potatoes, parsnips, swedes and turnips feature heavily in my Northern soup repertoire. I pluck fresh English herbs from my garden and make the most of *whatever* the butcher or the greengrocer recommends that day, or what's growing the garden – or even in the meadows and woods. We Northerners are soup experimenters because we are soup lovers and it's hard to pinpoint one particular Northern recipe because we've done them all and we'll continue to do so. That's the way cooking should be. Try out some of our Northern favourites in this book and you'll soon see what's possible.

It goes without saying that any soup, at any time of the year, needs a good old-fashioned side of fresh, warm bread and nice salty butter. Dip, mop and slurp it up. It's Northern cuisine at its finest.

SUPER STOCKS

Good-quality stocks are a key ingredient of delicious stews, casseroles, soups and pies, and they couldn't be easier to make. Up here we like to make the most of everything we cook, and stock is a great way to make use of carcasses and bones, and even leftovers. You'll find basic recipes below, all of which can be refrigerated for a week or frozen into ice-cube trays and used as required for three to four weeks. Don't hesitate to add your own favourite herbs and spices. Half the fun of home-cheffing is experimentation!

WHITE CHICKEN STOCK

This is a quite divine stock that can be used as a base for soups or nice light gravies.

MAKES 600ML STOCK

Chicken carcass and/or wings
2 carrots, peeled and chopped
1 onion, peeled and chopped
2 celery stalks, chopped
10 whole peppercorns
2 bay leaves
1 sprig of fresh rosemary
1 sprig of fresh thyme
1.2 litres water

In a large, heavy-bottomed pan, add all of the ingredients and cover with the water. Bring to the boil, and then simmer for 30–40 minutes. The stock should reduce by about half. Let it cool slightly, and then sieve to remove bones, herbs, spices and vegetables.

BROWN CHICKEN STOCK

The chicken has to be browned first so the flavours of this stock, and its colour, are deepened and intensified.

MAKES AROUND 1 LITRE STOCK

2kg raw chicken wings
3 tbsp vegetable oil
3 onions
3 carrots
1½ celery stalks
1 leek
500g tomatoes
1 tbsp tomato purée
1 bottle of dry white wine
3 litres boiling water
1 small bottle (185ml) of red wine
4 sprigs of fresh rosemary
4 sprigs of fresh thyme
2 bay leaves

Preheat the oven to 230°C/450°F/Gas mark 8.

Add the chicken wings to a roasting tin, rub with vegetable oil and throw in the oven on the top shelf for 30 minutes.

Roughly chop the onions, carrots, celery and leek without peeling and add to another large roasting dish. Take a ladle of the fat from the chicken wings, spoon over the vegetables and mix through.

Put the chicken back on the top shelf with the vegetables underneath and roast for 1 hour. After 40 minutes of that hour, throw the tomatoes and tomato purée onto the vegetables and cook until the vegetables and tomatoes are well browned, but not blackened. After this time, the chicken wings should be well browned too.

Take both roasting dishes from the oven, put the vegetable roasting tin over two rings of the hob and add the whole bottle of white wine. Scrape up all the caramelisation on the bottom of the tin. Add all the chicken wings and any caramelisation on the bottom of that tin to the vegetables and reduce the wine by half. Remove from the oven and tip the contents of the tray into a large, heavy-based stockpot.

Add the boiling water, the red wine and all the herbs, then bring to a low simmer, skimming as necessary, and cook, covered, on a very low heat for at least 6 hours.

Sieve all the ingredients from the stock and discard the ingredients.

Let cool and refrigerate overnight ideally, however, you could just continue from here by reducing by half (which you need to do after refrigeration too).

You now have your Brown Chicken Stock, which if left to cool or refrigerate will become a jelly as it is so concentrated. You can freeze this jelly as ice cubes for later use, then just flick 2–3 ice cubes into a gravy to transform the flavour.

BROWN BEEF STOCK

This is divine in soups, stews and even Northern-inspired Italian risottos!

MAKES AROUND 1 LITRE STOCK

500g trimmings of beef (ask for trimmings, if your butcher has them; if not, just let them know you need beef for a stock!)

2 pieces of beef bone, any size

2 carrots, unpeeled and chopped

3 onions, peeled and chopped

2 turnips, peeled and chopped

1 tbsp tomato purée

2 bay leaves

2 sprigs of fresh rosemary

2 sprigs of fresh thyme

4 fresh sage leaves

2.3 litres water

Preheat the oven to 180°C/350°F/Gas mark 4.

In a roasting tray, throw in your beef, beef bone, carrot, onion and turnip. Dab on your tomato purée and then place in the oven. Roast for about 45–60 minutes, until you have some nice deep colour. If you take it out too soon, your stock will be pale; if you leave it too late, you'll burn the lot!

Remove from the oven and tip the contents of the tray into a large, heavy-based stockpot. Add the bay leaves, rosemary, thyme and sage, and then cover with water.

Over high heat, bring to the boil. Reduce the heat and then simmer for 90 minutes, skimming frequently. Sieve the liquid, removing bones, meat, vegetables and any herbs, and then return to the pan. Cook, uncovered, for about 30 minutes or until the stock has reduced by about half.

LANCASHIRE PEA & HAM SOUP

Over the years, I have seen a lot of recipes for pea soup, most of which are delicate fresh-and-minty, English-country-garden affairs. Nice, but there is not a pea soup recipe out there to beat this robust, thick and creamy Northern adversary. It takes some planning and a little bit of patience, and be advised now that you'll need to leave the finished soup to stand overnight. But when the time comes, you can greedily devour it with Neolithic grunts and lashings of fine fresh, thick-sliced bread. In Lancashire everyone uses ham shank, but if you have trouble finding one, you can use ham hock instead.

SERVES AN ARMY!

450g dried marrowfat peas

1.5–2kg fresh ham shank (still a very cheap cut) or ham hock

2.25 litres water for the ham

2 celery stalks, finely chopped

3 carrots, peeled and chopped

2 onions, peeled and chopped

A few sprigs of fresh thyme

1 tsp cracked black peppercorns

2.25 litres water for the soup

1 tsp shop bought mint sauce

A small handful of fresh finely chopped parsley

There are two ways to prepare your dried marrowfat peas. Simply soak them in tepid water overnight (about 8 hours) or, alternatively, boil them up in a pan of water for 3 minutes, and then cover and simmer for a further 45 to 60 minutes until the peas are tender. Don't even think about eating raw soaked peas... (see Proper Mushy Peas on page 174).

Place your ham shank in a large, heavy-bottomed pan and add 2.25 litres water. Bring to the boil and turn the heat down to simmer for 10 minutes. Remove the ham and discard the water. This helps to desalinate the ham.

Place your ham shank, peas, celery, carrots, onions, thyme and black pepper in the pan, pour in another 2.25 litres water and bring to the boil. Cover and turn down the heat to create a nice slow simmer. Cook for 2 hours.

Remove the ham shank and set it aside to cool. Once cooled, discard the fat, take all the meat off the bone and cut into 2cm pieces. Put them back in the soup and liquidise half of it. Stir the liquidised soup into the remaining soup for a nice thick chunky texture.

66 When't winds blowin' a gale outside, put chickens in't coop ... 'N get stuck into a lovely thick pea 'n' ham soup!!

Cover and leave this gorgeous soup overnight in the fridge to enhance the flavours. It's a long wait, but believe me, it's well worth it.

Next day, reheat the soup for 15–20 minutes, stirring frequently to stop it sticking to the base of the pan. You may need to add a little water to loosen it. Finally, stir in the mint sauce and parsley. Check the seasoning only when it's finished, please.

OXTAIL SOUP

I once sat down to a *Coronation Street* lunch with all the cast to enjoy the sumptuous array of treats that were traditionally on offer. Barbara Knox (Rita Fairclough) was seated next to me and I asked her what she was thinking of eating. She immediately said, 'Oxtail soup and chips!' 'Together?' I asked. 'Oh yes,' she said demurely. 'Have you never tried soup and chips?' Hmmm. I tried it, but I still prefer my Oxtail Soup with a large chunk of brown bread and butter. I do like a woman who knows her own mind, though... The point of this story is that chips are optional!

SERVES 8

3 tbsp plain flour

1 tbsp mustard powder

1 tsp black pepper

A pinch of salt

1kg oxtail, jointed

4 tbsp groundnut oil

1 large carrot, peeled and roughly chopped

½ medium swede, peeled and roughly chopped

1 large red onion, peeled and roughly chopped

2 celery stalks, roughly chopped

2 tbsp tomato purée

275ml bottle of Mackeson's stout

Bouquet garni made of a sprig each of rosemary, thyme and sage tied round a celery stick

1 litre Brown Beef Stock (see pages 62-3)

2 bay leaves

2 tbsp Worcestershire sauce

1.8 litres water

In a mixing bowl, combine the flour, mustard powder, pepper and salt. Coat each piece of oxtail in the seasoned flour. Heat 2 tablespoons of the groundnut oil in a large heavy-bottomed pan until hot. Brown the oxtail on all sides, then remove from the pan and set aside.

Add the remaining groundnut oil to the pan, then throw in the carrot, swede, onion and celery and stir to mix. Add the tomato purée, Mackeson's and the bouquet garni. Stir to amalgamate for 2 minutes, then return the oxtail pieces to the pan with the stock, bay leaves, Worcestershire sauce and water. Bring to the boil, cover and simmer very gently for 2½–3 hours, skimming if necessary.

When the meat is falling off the bone, remove the oxtail. Strip the meat from the bones, then put it back in the soup. If the soup is too thin, reduce slightly, and if it's too thick, add a little bit more stock. Give it a good mix, check and adjust the seasoning – *et voilà!* This is the *real* thing.

ROASTED TOMATO SOUP

I used to be a Tomato Soup, Tomato Sauce kid, and I loved the stuff that came straight from a can or a bottle, but once you taste a proper tomato soup with carefully balanced flavours, you'll chuck all those cans of oozing red stuff in the bin once and for all. This recipe is the REAL version of a great British classic.

SERVES 4

1kg ripe tomatoes
1–2 garlic cloves, thinly sliced
A handful of fresh basil leaves
Pinch of sea salt
Olive oil
25g butter
2 onions, peeled and chopped
2 carrots, peeled and chopped
2 celery stalks, chopped
3 tbsp plain flour
1.5–1.75 litres chicken stock
2 small garlic cloves, peeled
  and chopped
3 good pinches of ground black
  pepper
1 tsp salt
1 tbsp soft light brown sugar
150ml single cream

Preheat the oven to 180°C/350°F/Gas 4.

Halve the tomatoes and place them in a baking dish. Put a thin slice of garlic and a basil leaf on top of each, sprinkle with sea salt and drizzle with olive oil, then cook in the oven for 30 minutes.

Meanwhile, melt the butter in a pan with 2 tbsp of the olive oil, add the onion, carrot and celery and cook over a medium heat, stirring occasionally, for 15 minutes until golden brown.

Add the flour and mix thoroughly with a wooden spoon off the heat.

Add the stock, chopped garlic, pepper, salt, sugar and the roasted tomatoes.

Cover and cook on the hob for 30 minutes over a medium heat, stirring occasionally. If a scum forms on the surface, skim it off.

Liquidise the soup in batches in a liquidiser, then push it through a sieve with the back of a spoon. Put into a fresh pan.

Pour in the cream and check the seasoning. You can bring it back to a simmer, but I usually serve mine lukewarm. The consistency should be good, but if it's too thick, just add more stock.

Serve with fresh chopped basil sprinkled on top, if you fancy, and a good chunk of white bread and butter. A sublime taste of summer!

SPRING VEGETABLE SOUP WITH LETTUCE

This is a very quick and wonderfully fresh-tasting soup that will impress any guest. I've been cooking it for years. As you can see from the ingredients list, 'finely chopped' is the key here, giving it a 'right sophisticated feel' (or whatever the Northern expression is) making it perfect for a light Saturday lunch or as a starter at a dinner party. Best of all, it takes only 10 minutes to cook!

SERVES 4–6

825ml chicken stock or water

1 tsp unsalted butter

1 shallot, peeled and finely chopped into 5mm cubes

1 small potato, peeled and finely chopped into 5mm cubes

1 small turnip, peeled and finely chopped into 5mm cubes

1 carrot, peeled and finely chopped into 5mm cubes

1 small courgette, finely chopped into 5mm cubes

1 small leek, washed, trimmed and finely sliced

1 tomato

4 iceberg lettuce leaves, torn in half

2 tbsp fresh chervil or dill, chopped (optional)

2 tbsp single cream

Juice of 1 lemon

Sea salt and freshly ground black pepper

In a large pan, bring your stock or water to the boil.

In a separate pan, melt your butter and 'sweat' your shallot, potato, turnip and carrot for 10 minutes until they have taken on a golden texture. Add your courgette and leek and cook for another minute. Season lightly. Tip your sautéed vegetables into the stock or water, reduce the heat and simmer for 8 minutes.

To peel the tomato, drop it into a pan of water that you've brought to the boil and leave for 3–4 minutes. When you puncture the skin with the tip of a sharp knife, it should shrink away and will peel off easily. Now finely chop.

When the vegetables are cooked, add the tomato, lettuce leaves and fresh herbs (if using) and stir in the single cream. Squeeze in a little lemon juice and that's it! Serve with crusty bread.

CULLEN SKINK

Cullen is a village on the Scottish Moray coast and this thick fish broth, or 'Skink', is the local speciality. We grew up on it down in Lancashire so I'm guessing it migrated down south with the fishing fleet because it's a real fisherman's soup. It's perfect for one of those 'comfort' days, and it's creamy, creamy, creamy, with a smoky undertone that really brings out the flavours of the fish. If you get your roux right, with not too much flour and a nice buttery, velvety consistency, it's about as easy as it gets.

SERVES 4

750g Finnan haddock fillets

2 large onions, peeled and roughly chopped

500g potatoes (a fluffy variety works well such as good old-fashioned King Edward baking potatoes, peeled and roughly chopped)

900ml full-fat milk

50g salted butter

50g plain flour, sieved

100ml single cream

Chopped fresh chives, to garnish

Sea salt and freshly ground black pepper, to taste

In a large soup pan, poach the haddock, onions and potatoes in the milk for 10 minutes until the fish is cooked. Strain and reserve the milk. Liquidise the strained fish, onion and potatoes in a liquidiser, adding a little of the milk if it is too thick.

Next, make the roux by melting the butter in a medium saucepan and carefully stirring in the flour, a little at a time. It's important to ensure that your roux is creamy, and not stodgy. Gradually add the reserved milk and beat vigorously with a whisk (not a fork) to produce a creamy béchamel sauce. Stir in the liquidised fish mixture and season to taste. Add as much cream as you wish to create a lovely, smooth soup. Reheat, taking care not to boil.

Serve steaming hot in soup bowls with a scattering of chopped chives on top. *Mmmmmm.*

LEEK & POTATO SOUP

From my point of view, Leek and Potato Soup should be silky, mellow, oniony and hot! There's nothing worse than lukewarm leek and potato soup. In fact, this soup should always be served so hot that you need to take care when eating it. I suggest cooking this whilst enjoying a glass of wine and savouring the amazing, homely smells coming from your kitchen!
I dare you not to feel completely sated by this soup and, best of all, it's super cheap to make. Leeks come in all shapes and sizes, pretty much all year round now, but the biggest and best soupy leeks are harvested in the autumn and winter, so keep an eye out for them!

SERVES 4–6

1kg leeks, washed and trimmed

75g salted butter

2 celery stalks, chopped

500g King Edward potatoes, peeled and roughly chopped into cubes

300ml full-fat milk

Sea salt and white pepper

4 tbsp single cream

1 knob of salted butter (optional)

Freshly chopped chives or dill, to garnish

Chop your leeks finely and give them a wash in a colander to get rid of any grit. Dry thoroughly on a clean tea towel. Melt your butter in a pan and add the chopped leek and celery. Cover and cook over a low heat for about 10 minutes to slowly soften the veg. Throw in your potato and stir, then add enough water to cover the potato. Bring to the boil, and then reduce the heat, simmering for 30 minutes.

Next, break up the potato with the back of a fork to make a nice, soft consistency. Add the milk and gently simmer for a further 30 minutes. Your house will soon be filled with a lush, leeky aroma! Season well with sea salt and ground white pepper and stir in the cream and a knob of butter for shininess, if desired. Liquidise it for a more refined soup, if you prefer. Give it a nice final swirl with your ladle and sprinkle with the chopped chives or dill.

Prepare a side of hearty brown bread and butter and enjoy! You'll make this soup again and again – I guarantee it!

BEYOND THE BAGEL

The influences on Northern grub from other cultures are many and varied, but few are as powerful as the Jewish tradition. After massive pogroms in Russia in the late nineteenth century, the UK's Jewish population expanded from around 46,000 in 1880 to some 250,000 by 1910, with many making their homes around Manchester and Leeds. With them they brought lots of the foods that we now consider Northern staples, and soup is just one of them.

The Jewish community has long understood the value of tucking into something warm, delicious and nurturing in both good and difficult times. There is a Yiddish saying, 'Worries go down better with soup than without'. Chicken soup (also known as the Jewish penicillin) is now one of our favourites up here in the North, served both with dumplings and without, and clouded with glistening chicken fat. Eastern European Jews were particularly creative with potatoes in soup, and this ever-present, inexpensive root vegetable is now the mainstay of many of our long-simmering soups, used to thicken and add bulk to a meal.

The Jews from Poland, Germany and other parts of Eastern Europe also helped to develop and expand our love of pickles. Preserving food was a characteristic of Eastern European cuisine, and we've acquired some fantastic recipes for pickling vegetables such as cabbage, beets, horseradish and cucumbers, as well as smoking fish and salting meat. Parsley, chives, dill and bay leaves were the preferred herbs in Eastern European Jewish cooking, and black pepper and paprika the most common spices. Take a gander through the recipes in this book and what do you see? Exactly.

The prohibition of work on the Jewish Sabbath (which runs from sundown on Friday till Saturday evening) meant they created slow-cooked, one-pot dishes (known as 'cholent') that needed little or no tending. A basic, traditional Jewish cholent is meat, potatoes, barley and beans. Sound familiar?

Our famous Oven-Bottom Muffins (see page 38) pay more than a tribute to the bagel, and given that there has been a solid Jewish community up here in the North since before the Middle Ages, it's perfectly possible that Jewish cooks had a hand in that too!

Jewish food is homely, hearty and intended to be shared – characteristics that warm a Northern heart and appeal to our sense of communality! Rumour has it that the Great British Fish 'n' Chips has its roots in Jewish fare too (see page 102) – I'll certainly take my hat off to Jewish cooking!

'Worries go down better with soup than without' goes the old Yiddish saying. I couldn't have said it better myself!

CHICKEN SOUP WITH DUMPLINGS

The North has a rich heritage of Jewish cuisine, first fairly exclusively within the Jewish community, but now very commonplace. This famous Jewish soup has many different variations, but we feel that this homely, traditional version reflects the beauty of good, simple Jewish fare.

SERVES 4–6

For the soup

1 free-range chicken, jointed into 8 pieces (skin on)

1 good-quality stock cube

3 carrots, peeled and diced

2 parsnips, peeled and diced

3 onions, peeled and diced

4 garlic cloves, finely chopped

1 or 2 leeks, washed, trimmed and sliced

A handful of chopped fresh parsley

A small handful of fresh dill

1 litre water

Sea salt and freshly ground black pepper

For the dumplings

2 eggs, separated

175g medium matzo meal (available in supermarkets)

3 tbsp vegetable oil

½ onion, chopped

2 garlic cloves, chopped

2 tbsp fresh parsley, chopped

1 tsp fresh sage (or dried will do), chopped

A couple of pinches of vegetable bouillon or ½ vegetable stock cube

Freshly ground black pepper

Place the chicken in a large pot and surround with the vegetables and herbs. Pour in the water, bring to the boil and then reduce the heat. Skim off any scum (this is important as whilst scum will continue to form, the first scum will potentially spoil the clarity and flavour of the soup). Add the stock cube and simmer, covered, for about 2 hours. Once cooked, you can skim off any fat, or alternatively, cool the soup and remove any fatty solids that have formed on the surface.

Remove the chicken with a slotted spoon. Cut or shred the chicken meat into chunks, discarding the skin and bones. Return the chicken to the pot with the vegetables and season. Return to the hob and continue to simmer while you make the dumplings.

To make the dumplings, first whisk the egg whites until they are stiff. Set aside.

In a mixing bowl, combine the egg yolks, matzo meal, oil, onion, garlic, herbs, black pepper and the vegetable bouillon. Give it a good stir and then fold in the egg whites. This will make the dumplings a little lighter and even more delicious! Cover the batter with cling film and chill for 30 minutes.

On the stove, boil a pan of water and prepare a bowl of cold water next to it. Dip a dessertspoon in the cold water and then into the batter. With wet hands, roll the batter into a perfect ball and then drop it into the boiling water. You should be able to make about 15–18 dumplings.

Once all the dumplings are in the water, cover the pan and cook for 15–20 minutes.

Remove the dumplings from the water with a slotted spoon and set aside for 10 minutes until they've firmed up.

To serve, reheat the soup and drop in the dumplings. Sprinkle with a little more parsley and black pepper if you wish.

Pies have been filling our bellies for *millennia*! Early pies (in the form of galettes, which had a casing made of ground oats, wheat, rye or barley round something tasty inside) first appeared when tools for grinding were developed in the Stone Age. We're talking 9500BC! As far back as 2000BC, the Ancient Egyptians created a rudimentary bread-like pastry, which they stuffed with nuts, honey and fruit, and a recipe for chicken pie was recorded on a tablet in Sumer, Mesopotamia, in 2000 BC. The Ancient Greeks made the whole thing official by inventing proper pie pastry sometime between 1400 and 600 BC. Because there was no refrigeration, they needed a way to preserve meat and they came up with a flour-and-water dough, which was wrapped around the meat to cook it and seal in the juices. In turn, it provided a lightweight container for long sea journeys and kept the contents a little fresher!

The Romans picked up the pie baton next, and pies became festive, somewhat more extravagant affairs – often a prize for victory in wars. These pies were large and had much more crust than filling. When the Romans paid their first visits to the UK, we acquired their skills, and developed a thick, hard and largely inedible crust known as a 'coffyn' (well, I suppose it contained a dead body), which acted as a bowl to hold the filling, rather than being a delicious part of the dish itself. In fact, crusts were often reused, over and over again, for a variety of different fillings, including whole birds, whose legs were left dangling over the sides.

Pies remained a staple for working and travelling people in the colder Northern European climes, and soon developed regional variations, like the Cornish pasty. The humble pie was an ingenious method of looking after a working man's daily food requirements, in an easy-to-transport form, offering plenty of good, filling protein inside and a whopping hit of carbohydrates in the crust. They were little packets of energy, and remain so to this day.

Up here in the North, we have a workforce who graft hard and need something substantial to satisfy appetites at the end of a hard day. It's colder up here, so we need stodge to keep the internal fires burning. The humble pie hits the nail on the head on all counts, and we now have hundreds of different pie recipes, developed over hundreds of years, to keep us going. They might be standard fare, but they are a *glorious* addition to Northern cuisine. I grew up craving pies, and barely a week goes by without a pie of some description taking pride of place on the family dining table. In my day, there weren't many Northern kids who wouldn't slyly keep their school dinner money for a chippy lunch, which, nine times out of ten, would include a delicious pie. We would even stick a pie inside a bread muffin to make what we called a 'Growler' – a pie 'butty'! We'd smother it in brown sauce and devour it in a few big bites before traipsing back to school. Happy days!

Your first taste of Northern grub has just got to be a pie, and we've given you plenty to choose from in this book. We've put a spin on some traditional favourites – adding caramelised onions to the Cheese 'n' Onion Pie, for example – and faithfully recreated others. The beauty of pies is that you can experiment to your heart's content, using up the contents of your fridge or whatever ingredient is seasonal or on special offer that day. You can use mince, fish, bacon and eggs, corned beef, veggies of every description for a family supper, or raise the bar and go for the more complicated game or raised pork pies – accompanied, of course, by a good old-fashioned gravy or Piccalilli!

Your basic pie dish is known as a 'plate' up here in the North, hence the term 'plate pies'. When God were a lad, housewives would make their pies in whatever ovenproof plate was available. Today, there is a whole gamut of choices when it comes to cooking pies, but we urge you to search out a nice, purpose-made, deep, ovenproof plate that is around 24cm in diameter and 4cm deep – or even bigger! Buy more than one, too. If you're anything like me, you'll have several on the go at any given time.

All this rhetoric may sound a bit serious for something as simple as a pie, but our travels around the North have showed us that the humble pie has a big and increasing following, and many people take the art of pie-making very seriously indeed. Pies may be plain comfort food for a hardworking family, but they are also the focus of competitions and awards, region after region after region. For example, every week, the Pork Pie Appreciation Society gathers at the historic Old Bridge Inn, Ripponden, West Yorkshire, where a designated person fetches a 'guest' pie and it's eaten and judged. Rejects are tossed to the ducks. It's a very serious business. And in Denby Dale, it's size that matters: they've been baking giant pies since 1788, when the first one was made to celebrate the recovery of King George III from madness. In 1966, the pie was 18 feet across and the barn in which it was made had to be demolished to get it out. The next one is featured in the TV series.

You don't need to go to extremes, though. The cooks of our beloved North have been conjuring up these dishes for a long time, and long may they continue. The pie's the limit!

Purists make pastry from scratch, but we time-stretched Northerners see nothing wrong with the shop-bought stuff from time to time.

PERFECT PASTRY

There are many gorgeous, traditional recipes for pastry in this book, and if time allows, it's well worth making the effort – and experiencing the pleasure – of doing it yourself! But, hey, I'm realistic, too. There are definitely times when a speedy alternative is required, and that's where shop bought pastry comes into its own. Some are actually very good. I sometimes cheat, but make sure I buy the best-quality ready-made pastry so that the resulting dish doesn't suffer in the taste and texture departments. For some of these recipes, I actually *suggest* shop bought varieties, for example, for Eccles Cakes (see page 32). The effort required to make your own puff pastry undermines the simplicity of this recipe, and I'm sure you'd rather make lots of these little nuggets of Lancashire heaven than keep them as an occasional, labour-intensive treat. Truth is, the shop bought pastry version of this recipe is (*shhhh...*) a lot more reliable! Filo pastry is a no-brainer. Shop bought is always the best alternative here; believe me, I've tried...

But when you do go DIY with pastry, it is possible to create perfection, if you bear in mind a few key tips.

Always keep your pastry as cool as possible. If your pastry is too soft when you are working it – or looks a little yellow, which means the fat has got too warm – stick the bowl in the fridge for a while to chill.

Try not to overwork your dough, which encourages the gluten in the flour to develop too quickly, leading to tough pastry.

Always sieve your flour, as the air will give your pastry a much lighter texture.

Allow your pastry to rest for at least 30 minutes in the fridge, to make it more elastic.

Don't leave out the salt, which enhances all of the other ingredients – even if it is just a pinch!

Always add liquid a little at a time. Too much liquid makes your pastry tough, and too little makes it oh-so crumbly.

Roll out your dough in one direction only, and rotate it to get an even shape.

When you're making a pie or tart case, always allow for the pastry to shrink as it's cooking.

Glazing your pie or tart with a little milk or beaten egg not only gives it a nice golden-brown finish, but it also helps to seal it, crisping it up in the process!

STEAK 'N' KIDNEY PIE

You won't have to wait long in any Northern chippy for someone to order this epitome of a traditional dish, with a side of chips, peas and gravy, of course! This pie really does typify the traditional North, through and through: like clogs and whippets, mills and cobbles. I'm sounding like that song 'Matchstick Men and Matchstick Cats and Dogs' by Brian and Michael now, but you know what I mean. You *must* try this dish.

SERVES 4

1 large handful of plain flour

1 tsp mustard powder

600g stewing beef (beef skirt is best), cut into cubes

150g ox kidney, cut into cubes

1 tbsp beef dripping or vegetable oil

1 onion, peeled and roughly chopped

440ml can of good dark ale (any kind, but not lager)

Bouquet garni made from 1 sprig each of fresh rosemary, bay, sage and thyme, all tied together

½ star anise

1 tbsp Worcestershire sauce

1 tsp tomato purée

1 quantity of shortcrust pastry (see Cheese 'n' Onion Pie page 90)

1 free-range egg, lightly beaten

Sea salt and freshly ground black pepper

Preheat the oven to 180°C/350°F/Gas mark 4. Season your flour with the mustard, salt and pepper. Rub the flour all over the meat. Place your beef in an ovenproof casserole dish, melt your beef dripping over high heat and brown your meat in batches. Set aside.

Turn down the heat to medium and add your onion. Sauté for about 5 minutes until golden, and scrape up all the 'gubbins' from the bottom of the pan. Return the meat to the dish and stir. Pour in enough beer to cover all of the ingredients and add your bouquet garni, star anise, Worcestershire sauce and tomato purée. Bring to the boil and skim. Cover and cook for a further 5 minutes on low heat. Transfer to the middle shelf of your oven and cook for 90 minutes.

While the filling is cooking, make your shortcrust pastry and let it rest in the fridge for 30 minutes. Split the dough into three pieces, then knead two of the pieces together and, on a floured surface, roll out a circle about 30cm across and 3mm thick. Grease a 26cm deep pie plate or dish. Now push the dough firmly into the bottom of the plate. Trim the edges of the dough.

When your meat is cooked, remove from the oven and season. Remove the bouquet garni and the star anise and then spoon the filling into the base of the plate. Roll out your remaining dough into a 3mm-thick round wide enough to cover the plate.

Paint the top edges of your pie base with beaten egg and then roll your lid over the top, sealing the edges with your thumb. Use the trimmings to make decorations if you wish. Paint the top with beaten egg, and make three slits in the middle of the lid.

Place in the middle of your oven for 40-50 minutes, until golden. Remove and allow to cool slightly.

CHICKEN PIE

Growing up in the North of England, chicken was a luxury and if we had a roast, it was made to last a week. There was certainly none of this breaded, battered stuff you find everywhere today. And when it came to chicken pies, the shop bought variety was as good as it got. If you ask me, when it comes to chicken pies, it's the gravy and shortcrust pastry version versus the creamy and puff pastry version. I experiment, refine and try to improve both – and here we have my creamy puff version. Don't worry about cheating with shop bought pastry; this dish should be a treat, not a chore.

SERVES 4

1 tbsp olive oil

50g butter

2 onions, peeled and finely chopped

2 carrots, peeled and finely chopped

2 leeks, washed, trimmed and finely chopped

4 garlic cloves, peeled and chopped

4 free-range chicken breasts

1 tbsp plain flour

A small glass of white wine

2 tsp Dijon mustard

1 tsp dried tarragon

1 tsp dried parsley

150g broad beans (fresh or cooked from frozen)

200ml milk

100ml double cream

A packet of ready-made pre-rolled puff pastry (made with butter, if possible)

1 egg

Sea salt and freshly ground black pepper

Preheat the oven to 180°C/350°F/Gas mark 4.

In a large pan, heat the olive oil and butter. Add the chopped vegetables and garlic and stir until they turn a lovely colour – about 5 minutes. Add a pinch of salt to help the process.

Meanwhile, chop your chicken breasts into large cubes and then add to the cooked vegetables. Stir and cook for another 5–10 minutes or until the chicken has taken on some colour too. At this stage, stir in the flour.

Add a glass of white wine, the Dijon mustard and the dried herbs. Stir thoroughly for a good couple of minutes.

Meanwhile, blanch your fresh broad beans for a minute in boiling water or cook your frozen beans for 3 minutes until they are soft. Drain and add to the chicken mixture.

Now add the milk and cream. Cook for another 5–10 minutes until the sauce has reduced and become nice and thick. If it's too thick just add a little more milk or cream. Pour the mixture into a suitable ovenware dish so that the mixture comes up to the top.

Cover the dish with your pre-rolled pastry, pressing down on the edge of the dish, and trim. Beat the egg and, with a kitchen brush, paint the pastry with the eggy mixture. This will give it a lovely glaze during cooking.

Bung it in the oven for 45 minutes or until the top is nice and crusty. Serve with seasonal veg and creamy mashed potatoes.

LANCASHIRE DEEP-PLATE PIE

Plate pies have been around in the North since the invention of plates. Everybody's mother made them and you could put anything in them. This is a great Northern pie with a *Great Northern Cookbook* twist of celery and garlic salts. This perfect pie is delicious warm, but is also divine served straight from the fridge with a pile of pickles on the side.

SERVES 4

2 tbsp groundnut oil

750g minced beef or beef skirt

4–6 shakes of Worcestershire sauce

1 tsp celery salt

1 tsp garlic salt

1 onion, peeled and roughly chopped

3 celery stalks, topped, tailed and roughly chopped

250g shortcrust pastry (shop bought or see Cheese 'n' Onion Pie page 90)

1 free-range egg, lightly beaten

Sea salt and white pepper

Gravy, to serve (made up from the recipe on page 90 with the addition of ½ chopped onion)

Preheat the oven to 180°C/350°F/Gas mark 4.

In a large frying pan, heat 1 tbsp of the groundnut oil till sizzling and add the beef. Over medium heat, cook your beef for about 10 minutes, stirring constantly and using a wooden spoon to separate the meat. Stir in about 4 to 6 dashes of Worcestershire sauce with the celery and garlic salts. Season to taste and set to one side.

In a large, lidded saucepan, heat the remaining groundnut oil and add the onion and celery. Turn down the heat to a very low simmer, put on the lid and cook for at least 20 minutes, shaking the pan from time to time. When they are cooked, stir in the beef and turn off the heat.

Split the dough into three pieces, then knead two of the three pieces together and, on a floured surface, roll out a circle to fit the base of a pie plate or dish that's roughly 20cm in diameter and 9cm deep. Now, offer up your pastry to the pie plate and push the dough firmly into the bottom. Trim the edges of the dough with a sharp knife.

Tip in the meat and vegetable mixture and then roll out another disc with the remaining pastry to create a top wide enough to cover the plate. Paint the top edges of your pie base with a little beaten egg or water, and then roll your lid over the top of the meat, carefully crimping or fluting the edges with the prongs of your finest fork (a great Northern tradition).

Use any leftover pastry trimmings to create decorations for the top then brush the top of the pie with the remainder of your beaten egg. Place in the oven and bake for 40–50 minutes, or until golden brown. Allow the pie to cool slightly before devouring with the gravy.

RAISED PORK PIE

Pork pies may have originated in the Midlands, but we in the North have adopted them as our own. Our version is made with hot-water pastry and baked in a high-sided sprung baking tin. I can imagine munching this whilst on the village green watching the local cricket team! Or, now I'm started, how about eating it down the pub, watching England play Germany, drinking real ale and dripping Piccalilli down your front?

SERVES 4–6

For the filling

700g pork belly, minced

300g smoked bacon, minced (this can be done by your friendly neighbourhood butcher)

1 tbsp sea salt

1 tbsp freshly ground black pepper

1 tbsp English mustard powder

2 tsp ground allspice

330ml water

230g pork fat (from the butcher)

1 sachet (7g) gelatine

For the hot-water pastry

500g plain flour

1 tsp salt

200g lard

110ml full-fat milk

110ml water

1 free-range egg, lightly beaten

In a large bowl, mix together the meat, salt, pepper, mustard and allspice and use your hands to mix thoroughly. In a small saucepan, bring the water to the boil and add the pork fat. Simmer for at least 60 minutes, uncovered. Pour the gelatine into the fat and water. Season generously with salt and remove from the heat.

Preheat the oven to 180°C/350°F/Gas mark 4, then make your pastry. Warm a mixing bowl and sift in the flour and salt. Make a well in the centre. In a small saucepan, heat the lard in your milk and water until just boiling. Pour into the well and stir quickly with a wooden spoon until thick. Next, get your hands in there and work the dough until smooth. Now you have to move quickly!

On a floured surface, roll out your pastry into a 40cm square. Grease an 18cm pie mould, and then carefully slip your hands under the pastry, lifting it gently into the mould. Delicately work the dough into the mould and trim off the excess pastry around the outside of the pie, to allow for shrinkage.

Place the meat mixture into the pie. Taking the excess pastry, roll out a lid. Secure the lid to the pie with beaten egg, firmly pinching together the lid and the base with your thumb and index finger. Liberally brush the top of the pie with your remaining egg.

Cut a small hole (about the size of a 5p coin) in the top of the pie. Bake for 30 minutes, and then reduce the heat to 160°C/320°F/Gas mark 3 and bake for a further 2 hours.

Remove from the oven and let the pie cool a little before adding the jelly to allow the meat to shrink and a space to form for the jelly. Pour your jelly mixture into the hole on the top of the pie until it pours out. Chill for 30 minutes. Eat cold with beer and Piccalilli (see page 204).

MEAT 'N' POTATO PIE

The Great Northern Meat 'n' Potato Pie is a classic dish that no Southerner can lay claim to. The most famous shop bought ones are Holland's Pies, made in Baxenden near Accrington. They've been in the pie business since 1851 and have become a beloved Northern institution with their green, red and gold delivery vans. However, you can't beat a homemade version and this recipe has been handed down through my family for generations.

SERVES 4–6

1 large handful of plain flour

1 tsp mustard powder

500g beef shin or stewing steak, cut into small cubes

2 tbsp groundnut oil or lard

1 onion, peeled and roughly chopped

2 carrots, peeled and cubed

1 litre water

8 sage leaves, finely chopped

1 bay leaf

3 tbsp Worcestershire sauce (optional)

1 quantity of shortcrust pastry (see Cheese 'n' Onion Pie page 90)

1kg good waxy potatoes, Charlotte or Maris Piper would be ideal, peeled and cut into 1.5cm chunky cubes

Sea salt and freshly ground white pepper

In a bowl, season your flour with the mustard powder, some sea salt and white pepper.

To make the filling, roll the beef cubes in the seasoned flour and set aside. In a large saucepan, heat the oil or lard until hot. Throw in the seasoned beef for a couple of minutes to colour, then add the onion and carrot and mix well. Add the water, sage, bay leaf and Worcestershire sauce, if using. Cover and bring to the boil, then skim. Turn down the heat to a slow simmer and cook for at least 2 hours.

While the filling is cooking, make your shortcrust pastry and chill for 30 minutes. Cook the potatoes for about 10 minutes until tender and then drain and cover with cold water to arrest the cooking process.

Preheat the oven to 180°C/350°F/Gas mark 4. When you are ready, split the pastry into two balls – one of two-thirds, the other a third – and roll out the larger one to a size that will easily cover the base of a 24cm diameter and 5cm deep pie dish. Grease your dish and then line it with the pastry and trim of the excess around the edges. Add the trimmings to your other piece of pastry and knead for a minute. Now roll out the top of the pie.

Drain the potatoes and add them to your beef, mixing and seasoning well. Carefully spoon the meat and potato mixture into the pie base, filling up the pie. Brush the edges of the base with a beaten egg and then lay the top on and seal the edges with a fork or your fingers. Glaze the pie liberally with beaten egg, pierce 3 holes in the middle and bake for 30 minutes until golden brown.

Serve a slice for each person, with Crinkle-Cut Chips (see page 172), Mushy Peas (see page 174) and a good brown gravy (see page 206).

ELSIE'S LUXURY LOBSTER PIE

My good friend Elsie Kerr was queen of the Newcastle supper party scene back in the seventies and her lobster pie was renowned. This dish definitely has a seventies feel to it, but it's a classic and at the same time a twist on your traditional fish pie. If you want to be fancy, use the best ingredients going. It's easy-peasy to make.

SERVES 4–6

1 medium-sized cooked lobster (about 100g meat)

50g butter

300g mixed white and undyed smoked fish (haddock preferably, but you can choose pollock or cod), skinned and cut into sizeable chunks

200g fresh shelled king prawns

1 large onion, peeled and finely chopped

1 tbsp flour

A handful of chopped fresh parsley

8 generous-sized floury potatoes, such as Whites, Desiree or King Edwards

A splash of milk or cream, for the potatoes

400g tin or bottle of shop bought lobster bisque soup

A big handful of breadcrumbs

A sprinkling of grated Parmesan cheese

Sea salt and freshly ground black pepper

Preheat the oven to 200°C/400°F/Gas mark 6.

Break open the lobster and remove the tail and claw meat, set aside.

In a large saucepan melt 25g of the butter, then add the chopped onions. Add a pinch of salt and sauté until golden.

Add the uncooked fish to the onions and cook for 5-7 minutes until the fish loses its translucency. Add the lobster and fresh parsley to the dish and another pinch of salt. Sieve in the flour and stir gently, being careful not to turn the fish into a mush!

Meanwhile, peel the potatoes and cut in half. Boil in a large pan of water until you can slide a knife into them, then drain. Mash the potatoes, adding a drop of milk (or cream) and the rest of the butter. Season with salt and pepper.

Add half of the bisque soup to the fish mixture and return to a low heat. The flour should stop it being too sloppy, but add a little more bisque if you need to. The sauce should cover the fish, but not too generously. Then transfer the mixture into a large casserole dish or ovenproof gratin dish. Taste and season the sauce again if necessary.

Cover the fish with the mashed potato. Sprinkle with breadcrumbs, then add some grated Parmesan cheese and dot with more butter.

Cook for 30 minutes until the top is golden brown and serve with green veg, such as sprouting broccoli and peas.

CHEESE 'N' ONION PIE

Cheese 'n' Onion Pie has to be up there as one of the mainstays of good, hearty 'Mothers' Fare'. We bring a little sweetness to the pie with the addition of caramelized onions, which perfectly balances the savoury Lancashire cheese. The beauty of this pie is its versatility – you can plate it up with mushy peas and gravy, or serve it cold for a picnic.

SERVES 4

For the filling

2 tbsp vegetable oil

4 onions, peeled and sliced

250g crumbly Lancashire cheese

Ground white pepper, to taste

For the shortcrust pastry

250g plain flour

A pinch of sea salt

50g unsalted butter and 50g lard (or 100g butter), at room temperature

A little milk, for brushing

1 free-range egg, beaten, for brushing

For the béchamel

25g salted butter

25g plain flour

250ml full-fat milk

Sea salt and ground white pepper, to taste

In a large pan with a tight-fitting lid, gently heat the oil. Add the onion, put on the lid, and turn down the heat as low as possible. Gently simmer for about 60 minutes, shaking the pan from time to time to prevent sticking.

To make the pastry, sift the flour and salt into a mixing bowl. Cut the butter and lard into cubes and add to the flour, then rub between your fingertips until you achieve a fine breadcrumb consistency. Gradually mix in cold water until all traces of flour are removed from the side of the bowl and your pastry is moist (not sticky or crumbly). Add more flour if it becomes too sticky and more water if it crumbles. Chuck your ball of pastry in a plastic bag and chill for 30 minutes.

To make the béchamel, in a small pan melt your butter over medium heat and sift in the flour. Stir together and cook gently for about 2 minutes to remove the 'floury' taste and achieve a nice 'wet' roux. Gradually whisk in the milk to create a smooth white sauce, continuing to beat until there are no lumps and your sauce has the consistency of double cream. Season, cover and set aside.

To make the pie, preheat the oven to 180°C/350°F/Gas mark 4. Split the pastry into two equal balls and roll one out as a base for your pie. Line a pie dish that's about 25cm in diameter and 4cm deep and trim off the excess around the edges. Crumble some of your cheese onto the base, sprinkle with white pepper and then cover with a layer of warm caramelised onions. Repeat in layers until all of your filling is in the tin.

Next, cover the pie with a good layer of béchamel and wet the top edges of your pastry with a little milk. Roll out the remaining pastry and cover the top of the pie, trimming the excess. Use a fork to seal the edges. Liberally wash the top of your pastry with beaten egg and cut two holes in the centre of the pie with a sharp knife. Bake in the middle of the oven for 40 minutes, or until golden.

FISH & SEAFOOD

In the North we are fortunate to enjoy a little present from Mother Nature – a narrow topography that gives us two very accessible coasts to choose from. And on these coasts are some of the finest fish and shellfish you're likely to find. It's only about 150 miles from Whitby in North Yorkshire to Morecambe in Lancashire, both of which combine spectacular coastlines with a wealth of seafood. We've got a shallow, sandy west coast, and a rocky, deep east coast, with their diverse array of species. Collectively they provide us with cod, haddock, saithe, plaice, sole, mackerel, herring, sprats and sand eels. And they offer an impressive range of crustaceans, including lobster, crab, brown shrimp, prawns, oysters, mussels and clams – a list worthy of any French port that gives us a king's banquet from the sea.

Fish and shellfish have always been a firm part of the Great Northern menu, and an important industry up here. Sadly, since the introduction of political quotas in the 1970s, every single one of our ports has suffered, and many fishing communities have been completely decimated as a result of these ever-tightening laws. It's hard on the people up here for various reasons, but there's no doubt that it's a good thing from an ecological angle. There has been a regrowth of fish and shellfish stocks as a result of being forced to dramatically reduce our takings from the seas.

Paradoxically, our Northern shores are now becoming increasingly famous for their produce – not just in the UK, but also around the world. We have the famous oysters from Lindisfarne; Whitby kippers and cod; and in Northumberland, we have crab and kippers from Craster, which also provides top-class lobster. In Morecambe Bay, with its shallow, sandy coastline, we have the beautiful brown shrimp and loads of flat fish, including plaice, dabs and fluke, a little known species with many local (and not-so-local) devotees. The rocky shoreline on the Yorkshire coast – in particular from Staithes to Spurn Point – provides some of the best brown crabs and lobster in the world. Such is the reputation, they're shipped across the globe and are eaten in the best restaurants in France and Spain.

Up here in the North, we have some fabulous exponents in the fine art of smoking fish and shellfish. The folk at the Port of Lancaster Smokehouse, in the village of Glasson Dock, produce a delicate, light smoke comparable to any of their famous European counterparts, and they have become firm friends over the years. Cedric Robinson, the Queen's Guide to Morecambe Bay, captivated Rev and me with tales of horse-drawn shrimping. Cedric has been plying his trade since 1950 and is still the only man entrusted with the job of guiding people over the treacherous mud flats of Morecambe Bay at low tide.

If you are a gastronaut, like me, you'll never fail to be excited by the discovery of new and vibrant places to source your food. Here in Manchester, I just love the fact that we have one of the best wet fish markets in the North – and maybe even the whole country. Even if I'm not on the prowl to purchase, it's a delight to see the diversity of fish and shellfish options available to the modern cook. In fact, some days, we only decide what to put on the menu after we've checked out what's fresh, new and interesting. With our local fishmongers, we get a chance to chat about how to do a particular fish justice, served with whatever's available from the greengrocer next door.

I actively encourage you to seek out your own local wet fish shop or fish market, and patronise them with your gastronomic pound. We home cooks set trends, and diversity increases with our demands. Spend wisely and never be afraid to quiz your local fishmonger about the freshest catch of the day. Ask him (or her) to trim and prepare your skate wing, and ask advice on recipes to enhance the wonderfully fresh fish and shellfish sold.

All of our fish and shellfish recipes have been prepared simply, retaining the freshness of the catch with the addition of only a few finely balanced ingredients. We're betting you'll cook these recipes again, and again, and again.

FLUKE WITH BUTTER & SHRIMP SAUCE

Anyone living near Morecambe Bay will be familiar with 'fluke', which is a flat fish that's slightly bigger than a dab and smaller than a plaice. The hardy fishermen who battle with the volatile elements on a daily basis to catch dab, plaice and shrimps have caught fluke in Morecambe Bay for generations. You can easily substitute dab for the fluke and not lose much of the essence of this dish. Cedric Robinson, who is nothing less than the Queen's Guide to Morecambe Bay – possibly the most treacherous expanse of sand in the country to an untrained walker – provided the inspiration that led me to create this recipe.

SERVES 4

4 fluke (or dab or plaice)

75g plain flour, seasoned with salt and pepper

2 tsp groundnut or vegetable oil

100g best unsalted butter

150g shelled shrimps (fresh, if possible, or cooked brown shrimps will do)

A splash of white wine vinegar

A squeeze of lemon juice

Finely chopped fresh parsley, to garnish

Sea salt and freshly ground black pepper to taste

Take your kitchen scissors and cut off the frilly end of the tail and the edges of the fluke (or dab), plus any fins. Pat dry and carefully roll each fish in your seasoned flour, dusting off any excess.

When all four fish are prepared, heat the oil in a frying pan with a knob of your butter until nice and hot. Place the fish in the frying pan or large saucepan and cook for about 3 to 4 minutes on each side, until golden brown. Remove the fish from the pan and place on a heated serving plate.

Add the remainder of the butter to the frying pan and bring it to a nice 'sizzle'. Add the shrimps, wine vinegar, lemon juice and salt and pepper, to taste.

To serve, drizzle your butter sauce over the fish, sprinkle with parsley and serve with new potatoes and seasonal greens.

SKATE WITH BLACK BUTTER

This recipe is a dark horse in every way. The finished dish is a perfect balance of fresh, beautiful skate wing, piquant capers and creamy browned butter. I emphasise the 'brown' because the aim is to produce a toasty-smelling, lovely brown butter, not something burnt or black! This is the king of seafood dishes and well worth the effort – every time! Serve with cracked new potatoes: Jersey Royals if they are in season.

SERVES 2

2 medium skate wings

1 litre water

1 onion, peeled and roughly chopped

2 celery stalks, roughly chopped

1 bay leaf

3 tbsp red wine vinegar

A pinch of sea salt

2–3 peppercorns (any colour)

75g unsalted butter

1 tbsp tiny capers

A sprinkling of finely chopped fresh parsley

Prepare your skate wings by chopping off the large bone at the bony end of the wing. With a large boning knife, slice along the bone (you will feel the angle to cut with your fingers). Then, with the knife in position, take an old rolling pin and hit the boning knife along the back of the blade. This will cleanly sever the bone from the wing. Next, use kitchen scissors to trim the frilly, wispy outer edge of the wing in a nice semi-circle. Only a few centimetres needs to be trimmed, and you'll know you've gone too far if you hit bone. If this all sounds too complicated, ask your fishmonger to do it for you or find a step-by-step tutorial on the internet (there are lots).

Next, add the water to your favourite large heavy-bottomed pan and stir in the onion, celery, bay leaf, red wine vinegar, salt and peppercorns. Bring to the boil and cook for 20 minutes. Add your skate wings, reduce the heat and simmer for 10 minutes. Carefully remove your skate with a fish slice and pat dry. Transfer the wings to a heated serving plate.

Melt the butter in a small saucepan until it becomes a pale golden brown and smells a little toasty. Tip in the capers and gently roll them in the butter, and then stir in the parsley. Spoon over the skate and serve immediately. This is a satisfying dish to make and the unbelievable flavours will make it worth every bit of effort!

SPICY MACKEREL WITH STRAWBERRY COMPOTE

On one of my many forays through Yorkshire when researching this book, Rev and I stopped off in Bradford for a light lunch of Tandoori Mackerel. As we savoured this tasty offering, we conjured up the idea of mixing Indian spices with the quintessential English strawberry! A stroke of genius. This is the result.

SERVES 4

4 medium fresh mackerel

80g salted butter, at room temperature

1 tbsp garam masala, plus a pinch

500g very ripe strawberries, trimmed and halved

3–4 slugs of balsamic vinegar

1 tbsp caster sugar

Snip off all of the fins and trim the tail of your mackerel with your kitchen scissors. With a sharp knife, slash each fillet four times diagonally, taking care not to go too deep.

In a small bowl, blend together your butter and garam masala until smooth. With your hands, smear it over the outside and inside of your mackerel, taking care to get it nice and deep into the slashes. Put to one side.

Next, prepare your compote by placing the strawberries, vinegar, sugar and the pinch of garam masala into a medium stainless steel pan, and cook over a medium heat for 5–8 minutes. Give it the odd stir.

While it's cooking, preheat your oven to 180°C/350°F/Gas mark 4.

Place all four mackerel on a roasting tray and cook on the top shelf of your oven for 15 to 18 minutes, or until the skin is nice and crispy. Serve on warmed plates with a tablespoon of delicious, spicy strawberry compote on the side. Plain rice and side salad are optional!

A little fishy on a little dishy when the curry boat comes in!

IRENE'S FINNAY HADDOCK

My mate Rev grew up with this dish in the late 1960s, when fish was still plentiful and, believe it or not, cheap! Irene, Rev's mum, would return from a hard day's work determined to get a good, quick and hearty meal together for the family, and she most certainly didn't fail. This is an inexpensive, unbelievably delicious dish that you can put together in no time flat. Finnan (we call it Finnay) haddock is traditionally caught in the North Sea and smoked in Aberdeen. Rev's mum served this with cracked new potatoes and seasonal greens, as her mum had before her. In fact, she still makes this dish on the Costa del Sol, as she fritters away Rev's inheritance.

SERVES 4

450ml full-fat milk

4 medium Finnan haddock fillets (if you can't find Finnan, go for the bright yellow rather than 'naturally smoked' stuff)

200g Lancashire crumbly cheese

Ground white pepper, to taste (no salt needed)

New potatoes and seasonal greens, to serve

Pour the milk into a large heavy-bottomed pan and bring to the boil. Lower the temperature until you have a lovely simmer and place your four Finnay haddocks gently into the milk. Poach for 5–7 minutes and remove with a fish slice onto a warmed place. Cover and set aside.

While the fish is cooking, grate or crumble your Lancashire cheese. Once the fish has been removed from the milk, stir in the cheese and simmer for a few minutes until you have a nice, creamy consistency. Add white pepper to taste.

Steam or boil your new potatoes and 'crack' them with a fork. Place the potatoes on a dish with the fish on top and then ladle over the delicious cheese sauce. Arrange the greens around the fish and potatoes. It doesn't get much better than this. Go on, take a bite.

FISH 'N' CHIPS

The first fish 'n' chip shop may have been opened in London by a Jewish immigrant, Joseph Malin, but chippies have a big long tradition up here in the North, and a fish 'n' chip supper remains a favourite weekly meal. Despite the fact that it was huge quantities of trawled fish from the North Sea that made this dish so cheap, popular and ubiquitous, fried fish first became popular in the South (Charles Dickens even mentions a 'fried fish warehouse' in *Oliver Twist*). However, it was in the North that we fine-tuned the art of frying 'chipped potato', which would soon accompany this Great British classic. Some think that fried chips became a substitute for fish up here when times were lean but it might have been our European neighbours, who brought the humble fried potato to our shores.

The two came together sometime around the middle of the nineteenth century, and the first Northern fish 'n' chip shop opened in Mossley market, Lancashire, two miles from where I was brought up. Whatever its roots, this dish was a sublime change from the typically bleak working-class diet and it instantly caught on. By the 1930s, there were more than 35,000 shops dotted around the country.

Chippies were packed on Friday evenings, when the weekly packet could be stretched to include a family treat and the religious tradition of eating fish on a Friday honoured!

Portions were often wrapped in old newspaper to keep down the prices (a practice that remained until the 1980s, when someone decided it was unsafe for food to come into contact with printer's ink), and if your budget didn't extend to a meal, it was possible to ask for 'scraps' – crispy batter leftovers that were not only free, but a staple indulgence for hungry Northern youngsters, who often picked up a bag on the way home from school.

We Northerners will stand up and be counted when it comes to finding the best fish 'n' chips in the land. Many of our chippies still use dripping or lard rather than vegetable oil for frying, which provides that extra depth of flavour, and we often use the finest Northern ales in our batter. We make the best mushy peas up here, too, laced with zesty malt vinegar, and we warm small pots of curry sauce or gravy to wet the chips. Brown sauce and tomato ketchup are acceptable to Northerners, but we draw the line at anything else!

It's claimed that this British favourite helped to raise morale during two world wars, and during the Second World War, ministers worked hard to ensure that fish and chips were one of the foods that were never rationed. The rest of the country may have bowed to pressure and made burgers, pizza, curries and Chinese the most popular takeaways, but in the North fish 'n' chips will always reign supreme.

POTTED SHRIMPS

The 'Legend of Morecambe Bay', 79-year-old Cedric Robinson, has been shrimping there for 63 years. In the past, he used his trusty black-and-white horse Trigger to harvest them, dragging the nets with water up to his nose! I was very fortunate to have the opportunity to eat such lovely fresh shrimps but, more importantly, to spend a day with the very fit Cedric on the volatile, sometimes dangerous, but nonetheless beautiful sands.

SERVES 6–8

500g fresh shrimps
150g salted butter
2 tsp anchovy essence
¼ tsp mace
¼ tsp cayenne pepper

Preheat the oven to 180°C/350°F/Gas mark 4.

Throw the shrimps in a pan of boiling water and cook for 2 minutes. Drain, allow them to cool, and then patiently remove them from their shells.

Melt 75g butter in a saucepan and stir in the anchovy essence, mace and cayenne pepper. Remove from the heat. Place the shrimps in a 20cm diameter ovenproof dish and pour over the seasoned butter. Place in the oven and bake for 30 minutes.

When the shrimps are done, remove from the oven and drain, reserving the butter. Leave to cool. Take six to eight ramekins or small containers and pack the cooled shrimps into them. Pour over the strained butter and refrigerate, leaving to set for 1–2 hours or, preferably, overnight.

Melt the remaining butter, pour on top and refrigerate for a further 30 minutes.

Serve with slices of brown bread, fresh or thin and lightly toasted. Smear with your delicious, buttery shrimps and devour with a cold Chardonnay or rosé.

SCALLOPS WITH LENTIL & CORIANDER SAUCE

This most beautiful recipe is the signature dish of one of my favourite chefs, Shaun Hill. He's won a multitude of awards, including two Michelin stars so I didn't think I'd be able to follow the recipe, but it's easier than you might think. Always use the freshest scallops you can find – not frozen – as it's the freshness of the shellfish that makes this dish.

SERVES 6 AS A STARTER

50g green lentils (no need to soak)

275ml stock, made from vegetable bouillon powder ideally

4 tsp groundnut oil

½ onion, peeled and finely chopped

1 garlic clove, peeled and crushed

2.5cm piece of ginger, peeled and finely grated

2 large, ripe tomatoes

2 tsp cardamom pods, seeds removed and husks discarded

50g best unsalted butter

1 level tbsp crème fraîche or double cream

Juice of ¼ lemon

20g fresh coriander, finely chopped, plus half a dozen sprigs to garnish

18 fresh scallops, cleaned with the corals attached

Sea salt and freshly ground black pepper

Rinse the lentils, then place them in a saucepan with the stock and simmer gently with the lid on for 40 minutes. Stir occasionally so that they don't stick to the bottom. They're ready when they're soft and breaking up. Drain the lentils and reserve the cooking liquid.

Take a frying pan and heat half the groundnut oil over a medium heat. Add the onion, garlic and grated ginger and fry for about 8 minutes until lightly golden.

To peel the tomatoes, drop them into a pan of water that you've brought to the boil and leave for 8–10 minutes. When you puncture the skin with the tip of a sharp knife, it will peel off easily. Now finely chop them and add them to the frying pan along with the cardamom seeds, two-thirds of the cooked lentils and all of the reserved cooking liquid. Pour into a food processor and whizz to a fine, but firm liquid. Add the remaining lentils and stir.

When you're ready to assemble the dish, reheat the lentil purée, whisk in the butter, the crème fraîche and lemon juice, and taste and season. Add the chopped coriander and keep the lentil mixture warm while you cook the scallops.

Heat a large non-stick frying pan over a high heat without adding the oil. Make sure the scallops are dry by patting them with kitchen paper. When the pan is searing hot brush the scallops with the remaining oil, season and add them to the pan. Without moving them around, cook them for about a minute. Once the underside has sealed and taken on a lovely caramelised colour, use a small palette knife to flip them over. Continue to cook for 30 seconds on the other side. To serve: scallops on plate, lentils on top or lentils on plate, scallops on top – the choice is yours. Garnish with the sprigs of coriander.

CRAB LINGUINE

Alban Donahoe has been a lifelong friend and drinking companion of both Rev and me since 'God were a lad'! Alban is a great home chef and has been a perfect host on the many times we have visited him and his lovely family. On one such visit, over a libation or two and a well-deserved catch-up, Alban threw together this simple, fresh, mouth-watering crab dish. Make sure you prepare this with your significant other and a glass of your favourite white wine to create just the right ambience!

SERVES 4

1 medium crab, cooked (from your fishmonger)

1 small chilli, deseeded and very finely chopped

Juice of 1 lime

A handful of coarsely grated ginger

2 tbsp coconut milk

500g dried linguine

Chopped fresh parsley to garnish

Sea salt and freshly ground black pepper

You'll need two bowls, two teaspoons and a rolling pin for this. With the face of the crab towards you, place your thumb onto the eye area, in the middle of the top of the crab. This should be slightly soft. Firmly grip the back of the crab with your fingers on the same hand. Now push your thumb firmly down and into the eye area, sliding it under the edge of the top shell and forcing it upwards. Your crab should now be open. Or you can ask your fishmonger to shell your crab for you!

Now, carefully search out the grey, frilly 'dead man's fingers' (which are not poisonous, by the way) that can be found just under the shell. Discard in one of the bowls, with the shell. Next, snap off the claws and set to one side.

Using one of your spoons, scoop out the crabmeat in the shell into your second bowl, using the handle of the spoon to reach any nooks and crannies. Next, take your rolling pin and gently crack open the claws, scraping out all that gorgeous white meat. Place in the bowl with the dark meat and pick through to make sure there are no bits of shell remaining. Discard the contents of your first bowl and any shell remaining.

Add the chilli and lime juice to the crabmeat. Gather up the ginger and squeeze it hard over the bowl to release its juices. Season and stir in the coconut milk. Mix thoroughly, cover and chill for at least 30 minutes to allow the flavours to merge.

When the crabmeat is ready, prepare a large pan of boiling water with a few pinches of sea salt. Add your linguine and cook, according to the instructions on the packet, until al dente. Drain and return to the pan with your crabmeat. Mix with two forks, to lift and separate the linguine and combine with the crab. If it seems a little dry, add a little more coconut milk. Serve immediately, sprinkled with parsley.

OYSTERS

Ah, fresh, briny oysters, served on a bed of cracked ice and topped with a sluice of Tabasco or fresh lemon. It's a taste experience that's impossible to define, and they slide straight down the throat in a rush of precious, tantalizingly flavourful liquor.

Jonathan Swift once said, "He was a bold man that first eat an oyster". Truth be told, we Northerners are as bold as brass, and oysters are not just native to our shores but an integral part of our culinary repertoire. We eat them fresh from the sea, nestled in their own shells, just hours after harvesting, and we don't mind putting aside a pound or two to get the best. A century or so ago, before supplies of oysters decreased, we bulked out our pies, soups and stews with the little critters, and we still pop them into a rich steak 'n' kidney pie or a savoury, gut-busting fish chowder, or serve the classic Angels on Horseback (oysters wrapped in bacon). We eat them hot, cold and warm but – and this is something you may not know – we always eat them alive. Yep, it's true. Whether you cook them or throw them back raw, an oyster needs to be alive and kicking up a storm in its shell before it hits your plate or frying pan.

On one of my missions with Rev to find the very best Northern ingredients, we stumbled across Lindisfarne Oyster Farm, on the site of the oyster beds established by the monks of the Lindisfarne Priory in Northumberland. Lindisfarne Oysters is a small, family-run business that recognizes the importance of growing high-quality oysters, and the beds were nothing short of magnificent. The oysters begin life in a wee hatchery. When they grow to the size of a thumbnail, they're transferred to the beds in the sea, where they lie in fine mesh bags on intertidal trestles. The amazingly pure, fresh waters off the shores of Lindisfarne provide them with oxygen and food and up to four years later, they reach maturity and can be harvested. The seas around our coasts are the perfect breeding ground for highly prized oysters, which filter and rely on sea water to survive.

According to Chris and Helen Sutherland, who run the Oystery, an oyster is a living animal and should be treated with care – kept cool and stored with the deeper cup on the bottom to preserve the outstandingly delicious liquor. They've got recipes galore, too, all tried and tested across their years of experience. Our mouths were watering at the thought of oysters poached in their own liquor, with a little white wine or water; lightly stir-fried with spring onion and ginger; grilled with cream, parmesan and freshly ground black pepper; or tossed in seasoned flour and fried in until golden. The best part? Washing it down with a glass of cold white wine or a frosty bottle of dark Northern ale. Now you're talking...

PRAWN CURRY

Tony Veg, a great mate, works at New Smithfield Market, the centre of the Northwest wholesale vegetable industry. Like me, Tony is a keen and passionate home chef and this recipe – an amalgamation of Indian and Thai recipes – is one of Tony's favourites. We first had this dish at his 'apartment', where we'd gathered to watch the Manchester Derby. It was Tony (the Blue) versus Rev and Sean (the Reds), but lo and behold, the Prawn Curry won! Enjoy.

SERVES 4–6

300ml chicken stock

1 bunch of spring onions, topped, tailed and chopped

½ tsp chilli flakes

5–6 Thai (bird's eye) red chillies

1 red pepper, seeds and white membrane removed, sliced

4 garlic cloves, peeled and chopped

4 tomatoes, quartered

1 tbsp fresh thyme leaves

1 tbsp Thai fish sauce

Juice of 1 lime

300g garlic butter sauce (packet sauce from the supermarket)

1 tbsp Madras curry paste

1kg fresh raw king prawns, peeled

2 tbsp fresh coriander, chopped

Sea salt and freshly ground black pepper

Preheat the oven to 150°C/300°F/Gas mark 2.

In a large casserole dish, bring your chicken stock to the boil, and then reduce to the lowest heat. Add your spring onion, chilli flakes and red chillies, and then stir in the red pepper and garlic. Add the quartered tomatoes, thyme, fish sauce and lime juice, stirring constantly. Stir in the garlic butter sauce and the Madras paste and check the seasoning. If the curry is too thick, add a little water.

Now, add the peeled prawns and cook through for 5 minutes. Remove from the hob and place in the oven for 60 minutes. When it's ready, garnish with the fresh coriander and serve with plain boiled rice. A cracking dish from a cracking bloke!

CASSEROLES, STEWS & CURRIES

You don't have to be an anthropologist to figure out that stews must have been the first example of one-pot cooking. Meat, foraged berries, herbs, foliage, mushrooms, vegetables and everything else 'in season' were thrown into a pot to bubble away over an open fire. Hitting the history books, Rev and I found out that in the fourth to eighth centuries BC, meat was placed in an animal's 'paunch', blended with water and 'boiled' over the bonfire. Not stew as we know it, but they got the idea. Turtle shells were used as early pots, then the Ancient Romans sorted out the metal business, hammering out receptacles that have withstood the test of centuries. They created cookery books, too, in a little series known as *Apicius*, with lamb and fish stews aplenty. The oldest French cookbook, hailing from the fourth century AD, has examples of ragouts and casseroles based on all sorts of meat, poultry and seafood.

We've noticed that the Northern stew has massive similarities to the French Provençal equivalent. For example, a French Pot-au-Feu (beef stew – neatly translated as 'pot on the fire'), with its shin beef, vegetables, herbs, bone and potatoes, has striking similarities to our very own Lancashire Hotpot. In fact, in a blind taste test it would be hard to choose between them. Consider, too, the Lob Scouse and the Irish Stew, which also have the same ingredients as Lancashire's finest hotpot. Each region has its own variations and traditions, with particular practices passing down from generation to generation, but it's the same basic meal.

For years and years, but especially during the post-war period, Northern casseroles were a regular part of the weekly diet. We relied upon these fabulous one-pot meals to make the best use of cheaper cuts of meat and to eke out smaller quantities of meat by creating magnificent gravies, dumplings and vegetables around them. In Sheffield, there's a tradition of serving stews piled onto pancakes, along with mashed spuds, carrots and gravy. Casseroling and stewing (note: it's a casserole if it's done in the oven and a stew if it's cooked on the hob) are the ideal vehicles for cheaper meats, which need to cook for much longer to break down the gelatinous marbling and the stringier connective tissue. There can be nothing tastier than a wonderful slow-cooked meat, falling away from the bone or shredding itself into the divinely flavoured liquid that it's cooked in.

There was also the issue of energy. Hearty casseroles not only satisfied big appetites, and provided grafters with warm, nourishing meals to energise, but they were easy to make because they're cooked slowly over low heats and don't need much attention once you've chucked everything in the pot. Best of all, a big casserole would last a family two days (at least), so it's not surprising that they became a Northern favourite. It was always on the second day that casseroles came into their own, after the ingredients had had time to deepen and amalgamate, and the meat was softer than ever. Let's just say that if you haven't tried spreading your stews across two days, you should.

How do you sum up a good Northern casserole? Cheap as chips and with a taste to die for. Casseroles can be thickened (and made hardier) by reduction, of course, but also by coating your meat in seasoned flour or using a 'roux' (equal parts of butter and flour). We like things thick in the North, and most of our stews, soups and casseroles will hold an upright spoon – easily!

We cannot, absolutely cannot, forget the Asian influences up here too. We have a fabulous Asian community in the North, and they've not only brought with them the same frugal, budget-conscious cooking in their amazing curry dishes, but they've introduced us to a wealth of fragrant spices, not to mention pulses. If anyone knows how to eke out a good meal and make it even more delicious and nutritious, it's our Asian compatriots. Like we do, they enhance a hearty one-pot stew with a range of carbohydrate fillers. In their case, it's chapattis or parathas; in ours, it's pastry, dumplings and lashings of bread and butter. We'd like to point out that we're eating more and more of theirs, too (see page 128)!

Our casseroles are regional and undoubtedly have cultural variations, but they are all cooked with pride, have the tastiest gravy known to man and keep you going day after day after day. Leave them to simmer away while you head off to work or play with the kids, and you'll have a meal fit for a king upon your return. We guarantee it.

BEEF STEW WITH DUMPLINGS

There are many takes on this deliciously rich beef stew, and every Northerner has his or her own favourite version. This one ignores the traditional 'bouquet garni', red wine, balsamic vinegars and highfalutin stuff. Here we've gone back to basics with good, honest ingredients cooked in that great Northern way. Quite simply, the results speak for themselves! Truly a stew like no other: simple, quick, filling and quite simply delicious!

SERVES 4–6

For the stew

750g beef shin or good-quality stewing steak

1 tbsp plain flour

1 tsp mustard powder

40g beef dripping or vegetable oil

4 small onions, peeled and diced

900ml water

4 carrots, peeled and cut into 4 chunks

2 swedes, peeled and cubed

2 celery stalks, finely diced

3 bay leaves

Sea salt and freshly ground black pepper

For the dumplings

175g self-raising flour

75g shredded suet

A good pinch of sea salt and freshly ground black or white pepper

There's stewing steak and stewing steak. If you can get your butcher to give you the best, all the better. Carefully remove any gristle and fat from the meat and trim into neat 4cm cubes. Spoon the flour and mustard powder into a bowl and drop in the meat, coating it with the seasoning.

Heat the dripping or oil in a pan. Brown the beef, then add the onion and cook until both take on a good colour. Season with salt and pepper. Stir in the water and bring to the boil. Season again to taste, cover and gently simmer for 60 minutes. Add the carrot, swede, celery and bay leaves and simmer for a further 90 minutes.

Meanwhile, sieve the flour for the dumplings into a bowl and add the suet, salt and pepper. Slowly add 3 tbsp water to the mix to create a soft, but not sticky dough. If you overdo it, add a wee bit more flour to even things out.

Lightly flour your hands and roll the dough into eight small balls. Drop them carefully into the stew, cover the pot, and cook for a further 15–20 minutes. Your dumplings should be plump and moist, but definitely cooked all the way through.

Serve in a lovely bowl with a side of crusty bread and maybe even a light green salad.

STEAK, OYSTER & ALE PUDDING

Back in the 1800s, when oysters were plentiful and not the expensive delicacy they are now, this pudding was a Great Northern staple. I was thinking about developing a steak and oyster pie recipe when Rev and I went on a visit to a local brewery, tasted their ale and it was a 'Eureka' moment! Both being lovers of seafood and ale, well, we couldn't resist! Piping hot beef with the natural saltiness of the oysters and ale gravy really makes this a Yorkshire classic.

SERVES 4

A knob of beef dripping or a splash of vegetable oil

500g beef shin or stewing steak, diced small

2 onions, peeled and chopped

1 heaped tbsp tomato purée

1 tbsp Worcestershire sauce

40g plain flour

440ml can of stout

Bouquet garni made from 1 celery stalk and 1 sprig each of fresh rosemary, sage and thyme, all tied together

4 oysters

1 free-range egg, beaten

Sea salt and freshly ground black pepper

For the pastry

200g box of vegetable suet

400g self-raising flour

1 tsp salt (optional)

10–12 tbsp water

In a large heavy-bottomed pan, melt your beef dripping or heat your vegetable oil and brown the meat, then remove. Fry the onion with a little salt for about 20 minutes, scraping up the brown sticky bits from the bottom of the pan. Put the meat back in with the tomato purée, Worcestershire sauce and flour and cook for 3 minutes. Add half of the stout and stir for a minute to amalgamate, then add the rest of the beer along with the bouquet garni. Stir then simmer for an hour, stirring from time to time.

Pour in any juices from the oysters and season to taste. Leave to cool.

Mix the dry pastry ingredients, then add the water, spoonful by spoonful, until you have a dough that is smooth but not sticky. Divide your pastry into two portions, of two-thirds and a third. Roll the bigger one out to a circle that's 4–5mm thick. Slide it over your rolling pin, then transfer it to a 1.5-litre pudding bowl. Press it down to line the base of the bowl and trim the edges. Add a quarter of the meat and sauce, then two oysters, in alternate layers, and finish with the remaining meat. Roll out the rest of the pastry to make a lid and put it in place, trimming the edges. Crimp the edges and seal the pastry with a little beaten egg. Cover tightly with foil, tying it in place with a piece of string. Place it in a pan with a litre of boiling water and steam for 3 hours.

When it's done, let the pudding cool for 5 minutes then, using towels or oven gloves on your hands, lift the bowl and upend your pudding onto a plate.

Serve with Proper Mushy Peas (see page 174) and buttered mash.

CHILLI CON CARNE

Lots of spices arrived in Liverpool from the Caribbean and gave us Northerners a taste for spicy food. A really good Chilli Con Carne is not difficult to make, but how often can we *truly* say that we just ate a 'great' chilli? This recipe is guaranteed to lay that anomaly to rest. Incidentally, authentic Chilli Con Carne does not have red kidney beans mixed in with the meat. They are usually served as a separate side dish, but how you serve them is up to you. Do note that you'll need some chilling time before reheating and serving to get the best result. Factor that in, if you can bear it.

SERVES 8

2 tbsp olive oil

75g pancetta, diced

1 large mild onion, finely chopped

4 garlic cloves, finely chopped

750g stewing steak, cut into small cubes

250g pork belly, cut into small cubes

3 tbsp Mexican chilli powder (not too hot!)

1 tbsp ground cumin

1 tbsp plain flour

2 bay leaves

1 lemon, peeled, seeded and finely chopped

1 tbsp dried oregano

4 ripe tomatoes

450ml good-quality beef or chicken stock

375ml good-quality red wine

400g tin of red kidney beans, drained

A small bunch of fresh flat leaf parsley, chopped, to garnish

Juice of 1 lime (optional)

Sea salt

In a large flameproof casserole dish, heat a little olive oil and gently cook your pancetta till crisp and brown. Add the chopped onion and garlic, cooking for a few minutes until they start to brown. I love the smell at this stage! Remove from the pan and, in the residual oil, brown the stewing steak and pork belly (in batches, if necessary).

When all the meat has been browned, add the chilli powder and cumin and cook for 2 further minutes, stirring to avoid the contents sticking. Now sprinkle in the flour and cook for another minute. Return the onion and pancetta to the pan and add the bay leaves, salt, chopped lemon, oregano, tomatoes, beef stock and red wine.

Over a gentle heat, bring everything to a simmer and continue to cook, uncovered, for a minimum of 2 hours. If you do want to add your kidney beans to the meat, add them about halfway through the cooking time. The sauce will thicken and most of the liquid will reduce. The meat will turn a lovely dark colour and almost literally fall apart into tender shreds. Allow to cool completely before covering and refrigerating for up to 48 hours. Remove from the fridge and skim off any excess fat.

Now, reheat gently, add the parsley and perhaps a quick squeeze of lime juice and serve with a flourish. This recipe is delicious with rice, boiled potatoes or, my favourite, spooned into warmed pitta bread and served with a dollop of sour cream.

TAITERASH

Including this recipe in the book was a close call: *everyone* in the North knows how to make a good Taiterash! If you aren't yet acquainted with the 'dark art' of creating a crackin' Northern Taiterash, this one's for you. Let's just say that it's popular because it's *gorgeous*! Don't forget the accompanying pickles – they are as essential to the dish as cold malt vinegar is to fish 'n' chips! Of course, the whole lot needs mopping up with lashings of bread.

SERVES AN ARMY

70g plain flour

1kg stewing beef or beef skirt, cut into 2.5cm cubes

2 tbsp groundnut oil

2 onions, peeled and roughly chopped

3 carrots, peeled and quartered

1.25kg King Edward potatoes, peeled and cut into 2.5cm cubes

2 beef stock cubes

Bouquet garni made from 1 celery stalk and 1 sprig each of fresh rosemary, sage and thyme, all tied together

Lancashire relish or Worcestershire sauce

Sea salt and freshly ground white pepper

Season your flour with salt and pepper and use it to rub your meat until well coated. In your favourite stockpot, heat the groundnut oil and chuck in the meat. Using a wooden spoon, agitate the meat to ensure that it's nicely browned on all sides. This adds flavour! Remove the meat with a slotted spoon and set to one side.

Add the onion to the pan to deglaze, scraping up all the good bits from the bottom of the pan. Turn the heat down to medium and throw in the carrot. Cook for 3 minutes, and then add the potato cubes and cook for a further 2 minutes. Stir constantly. Take the pan off the heat and crumble in your stock cubes, stirring through. Return the meat to the pan. Pour in enough water to cover all of the ingredients, and then add the bouquet garni and relish or Worcestershire sauce.

Cover and simmer on your lowest heat for 90 minutes, stirring occasionally. From time to time use the back of a fork to help break down some of the potato. When it's done, your hash should be full of half-dropped potatoes and nearly stringy meat, with some of the potatoes broken down to thicken the dish. Season with sea salt and white pepper, to taste.

Serve with pickled red cabbage or beetroot (or both). That's the traditional way, folks!

OX CHEEK CASSEROLE

Rev and I were wandering round Lancashire's Clitheroe market, getting to know the place, when a cheery butcher introduced us to ox cheeks. We bought two, at 600g each, and they only cost us a fiver, which is really cheap for meat. I came home to invent a recipe for them and because they have a rich flavour, I counterbalanced that with orange juice – beef and orange are a classic combination – throwing in some root veg too for a handy one-pot dinner.

SERVES 4

70g plain flour

2 ox cheeks, cubed

2 tbsp groundnut oil

1 tsp butter

4 rashers of smoked bacon, chopped into 2.5cm squares

3–4 shallots, peeled and roughly chopped

4 garlic cloves, peeled and chopped

3 carrots, peeled, halved lengthways and chopped

3 nasturtium roots, sliced into 1cm chunks (if you can't get these, use 4 medium turnips, quartered)

½ bottle of red wine

1 sprig each of fresh thyme and rosemary

1 bay leaf

3 blood oranges

Sea salt and freshly ground white pepper

Season your flour in a bowl with salt and pepper, drop in your ox cheeks and coat. Shake off any excess. Next, heat 1 tablespoon of your oil and the butter in a pan over high heat and 'seal' the ox cheeks until they are nice and brown. Place on a plate and set to one side.

In a large flameproof casserole pan or dish, heat your remaining groundnut oil and tip in the bacon. Cook until nice and brown, and then add the shallot, garlic, carrot and nasturtium roots, stirring until beginning to soften. Add the ox cheeks, red wine, thyme, rosemary and bay leaf and pour in enough water to cover.

Quarter your blood oranges and squeeze in the juice from all but one quarter. Add this final unsqueezed quarter to the pot.

Cook for 2½ to 3 hours and then remove the herbs and orange quarter. Season with sea salt and white pepper, to taste. Serve in big white bowls with crusty bread and devour!

LANCASHIRE HOTPOT

Many, many years ago, when the bakers of small Lancashire villages finished their shifts and turned off the ovens, the good village people would prepare this hearty dish and whip it round to the bakery to make use of an oven temperature that was tailor-made for a slowly simmering hotpot. The villagers then went about their daily chores until this traditional Lancashire dish was simmered to perfection. Some prefer it without the kidneys, but I prefer it with.

SERVES 4 (AT LEAST!)

1 tbsp groundnut oil

6 x 2.5cm-thick lamb neck chops

5 large potatoes, peeled and thinly sliced, and then steeped in fresh, cold water

1 large onion, peeled and thinly sliced

2 carrots, peeled and cubed

2 prepared lamb's kidneys, thinly sliced (optional)

2 sprigs of fresh thyme

1 sprig of fresh rosemary

2 litres chicken stock

Sea salt and freshly ground black pepper

Preheat the oven to 180°C/350°F/Gas mark 4.

In a heavy-bottomed frying pan, heat your groundnut oil and cook your lamb chops until nicely browned. Remove from the pan and set to one side.

In the bottom of your favourite, lidded casserole dish, spread a single layer of overlapping slices of potato. Sprinkle with a third of the onion, carrot and the kidneys (if using) and then top with two browned chops. Season this layer, and repeat the process twice more, covering with potato, onion, carrot, kidney (if using) and two chops. Season again, and lay your herbs over the top.

Now, cover the entire dish with the remaining potato, overlapping the slices to make an attractive arrangement. Carefully pour over two-thirds of your chicken stock, which should come to the top of the dish.

Cover, place in the middle of your oven, and cook for 2 hours. Remove from the oven, pour over your remaining chicken stock and return to the oven for another 30 minutes. When your hotpot is ready, remove from the oven and carefully pull out your herbs. Serve with brown bread on the side to mop up the juices and then devour!

LOB SCOUSE

The word 'scouse' comes from *Lobscouse* (originally 'lob's course') or *labskaus*, meaning 'stew', and refers to a meat-based stew commonly eaten by sailors throughout Northern Europe. Norwegian sailors brought it to Liverpool, where it became so popular that over the years 'scouse' became a nickname for Liverpudlians. It's basically their version of the Lancashire Hotpot. I find it amazing that fifty miles can change a recipe completely – not to mention an accent!

SERVES 4

4–6 neck chops (it wouldn't be a Lob Scouse with any other cut, but you could use lamb chops on the bone if really can't get neck chops)

1 tbsp groundnut oil

2 large carrots, peeled and sliced

1 large onion, peeled and chopped

2–3 celery stalks, plus leaves, chopped

500ml chicken stock (from a cube is fine)

2 bay leaves

6 large potatoes (Cyprus work well here), peeled and cut into 2cm slices

Cut off any fat from the edges of the lamb chops and finely slice the fat. Add your groundnut oil to a frying and turn the heat to medium. Add the sliced fat and cook until it is 'rendered' or slightly melted, leaving a good lamb-flavoured oil with which to proceed. Remove any remaining pieces of fat with a slotted spoon and lightly brown your chops.

Add the carrot, onion and celery and cover with stock. Pop in your bay leaves and add enough water to ensure that all of your ingredients are covered. Bring to the boil and then simmer until your carrot begins to soften. Add your potato and cook, uncovered, for about an hour. Keep an eye on the pan and take it off the heat when the potatoes start to 'lob' (fall apart). Whatever you do, avoid letting the potatoes turn into mush.

Remove the bay leaves and gently stir the ingredients together, taking care not to crush the potato. Serve immediately with red cabbage or preserved beetroot for a traditional, delicious meal!

As they say in Liverpool, 'It's the gear!'

LAMB 'N' BEANS

Every home cook needs a handful of one-pot recipes that can be thrown together at the last minute and slammed into the oven for a quick-and-easy meal. This recipe fits the bill perfectly, and the taste is quite simply sensational! As you might have guessed, I do love a chop – it gives a depth to the flavour and the best thing is you can pick it up and nibble it. But if you want, substitute the lamb chops for lamb shoulder or diced lamb, such as can be found in any supermarket. Lamb 'n' Beans is a hearty standby up here in the North and I'm sure you'll love it as much as I do.

SERVES 4

4 lamb neck chops

1–2 tbsp groundnut oil

Bouquet garni made from 1 celery stalk and 2–3 sprigs of fresh rosemary and thyme, all tied together

3 bay leaves

5 black peppercorns

Sea salt

2 large carrots, peeled and quartered

8 shallots, peeled and halved

3 turnips, peeled and quartered

2 leeks, washed, trimmed and cut into 2.5cm pieces

A handful of soup and broth mix (a mixture of pearl barley and lentils)

400g tin of borlotti beans (with their liquid)

1 tsp mint sauce

Preheat the oven to 180°C/350°F/Gas mark 4.

In a large pan, brown the lamb in the groundnut oil. Add the bouquet garni, bay leaves, peppercorns and a pinch of salt. Cover with water and bring to the boil. Cook for 5 minutes on a high heat, skimming regularly, and then reduce to a gentle simmer. Stir in the vegetables and broth mix, and then transfer the whole lot to your favourite casserole dish, cover and cook in the oven for 60 minutes.

When it's cooked, remove the dish from the oven, mix thoroughly, add the borlotti beans and liquid and swirl in the mint sauce. Season to taste. Leave to stand for 2 minutes to let the beans warm through. Scoff with loads of crusty bread and listen to the silence of...the lambs.

RABBIT, LEEK & TARRAGON CASSEROLE

Rabbit must be the most underrated meat around in the twenty-first century, but it used to be a very popular pie filling up North in the eighteenth and nineteenth centuries because it was much cheaper than beef. And there's nothing like a good rabbit casserole. This one is dead posh, but then it comes from my mate Richard who is! He likes the saddle because it's white meat and not gamey, and for rabbit beginners that's a great cut to start with. Your butcher is your best bet for rabbit – and whether it's saddle, or the whole animal, the price should be roughly the same.

SERVES 3-4

A whole farmed rabbit, cut into 7 pieces (2 x shoulders, 2 x legs, 3 x saddle) or 2–3 rabbits and just use the 6 saddle pieces

Plain flour, for dusting

25g best unsalted butter

1 onion, peeled and finely chopped

2 leeks, washed, trimmed and finely chopped

Splash of olive oil

4 garlic cloves, finely chopped

2 fresh sage leaves

4 sprigs of fresh tarragon or 3 tbsp dried tarragon

1 tbsp good-quality English mustard

200ml dry white wine

150ml lamb stock

100ml single cream

Sea salt and freshly ground black pepper

Preheat the oven to 200°C/400°F/Gas mark 6.

Gently dust the rabbit pieces with plain flour. Place a large, heavy-based casserole dish on a medium heat, melt the butter and once lightly bubbling, add the onion and leek. Season with the salt and cook until soft and golden.

In a separate pan, heat a splash of olive oil and add the rabbit pieces, season with a pinch of salt and 4 pinches of ground black pepper and cook for 7–8 minutes until nicely golden on all sides. Add the garlic, sage and tarragon and cook until wilted. Add a tablespoon of mustard. Stir in so everything is coated.

Add the wine and lamb stock to the rabbit and bring to the boil until all the brown bits on the bottom of the pan scrape off.

Combine the rabbit and juices with the cooked leek and onion in the casserole dish, put the lid on it and place in the oven for an hour. If you are cooking just the saddle, you will probably need less cooking time. Three quarters of an hour should do it.

To serve, remove the meat from the casserole dish and keep warm on a plate in the oven. On the stove, reduce the liquid by one-third, stirring regularly. Reduce the heat and add the single cream, warm and then ladle the sauce over the rabbit. Serve with new potatoes and seasonal vegetables.

SOME LIKE IT HOT!

Asian influences on Northern food abound, and we've taken to curries and other Indian dishes like fish to water. In fact, in 2011, Bradford in Yorkshire was crowned curry capital of the UK. When we like something, we do it *right!* Waves of immigrants from Asia (the South in particular) began entering the UK when the East India Company arrived on the Indian subcontinent, and a steady stream continued over the coming years, particularly after the independence of India, Pakistan, Bangladesh and Sri Lanka from British rule. Manual workers, mainly from Pakistan, were recruited after the Second World War, when labour was short, and many settled here to work the night shifts in factories and mills.

By the 1940s, curry houses began to spring up, serving Indian street food. It wasn't long before students realised that the flavour and the value was second to none, and soon droves of Northerners were visiting curry restaurants on a regular basis. The growing demand for a good 'vindaloo' created a wealth of jobs in the catering industry and we fell in love! Heading out for a curry became a national pastime, and Indian home cookery also abounded.

There had, however, been steady, more subtle influences on our Northern cuisine for many years. In fact, from the 1700s, we slowly started adding Indian herbs to our recipes, and creating more dishes based on rice. Salt, peppercorns, lemon juice and coriander seeds made an appearance, and by the nineteenth century, we were using ginger, cayenne, turmeric, cumin and fenugreek. Yoghurt, coconut and almonds were eventually introduced to Northern meals, and we began to season our chutneys with limes, mangos, cardamom and chillies. Piccalilli is an early English attempt at Indian pickle!

Although the Northern diet was dominated by red meat, accompanied by home-grownveg like cabbage and potatoes, we were learning to spice it up. We also learned to be more inventive with vegetables, using traditional English favourites like root vegetables and cauliflower in Indian curries. Our passion for penny-pinching meant that we could spot a bargain a mile off, and Indian food represented just that. In fact, a fusion of our one-pot meal ideology with the Asian curry pan created some of the finest Northern meals today. No waste, no mess, and lashings of good bread (naan or white bloomer) on the side.

We're a little more adventurous now, and we're popping lentils and spices into our traditional casseroles like there's no tomorrow. We've got an obsession with curry and spicy sauces, and our commitment to condiments is legendary. Indian food is now an intrinsic part of our cuisine and we, for one, like it hot!

Whatever way you look at it, Asian influences on Northern cuisine are undoubtedly a recipe for success.

LEMONY CORIANDERY CHICKEN

This is a dish that I have cooked for years and years, and it also happens to be my son Callum's absolute, all-time favourite. It's so easy to make and fragrant beyond belief – a must-try for the whole family. Callum loves sucking on the chicken bones, so if your kids are anything like mine, you'll need to keep a tea towel to hand to wipe those chops! Serve with your own spiced rice and some chapattis: *Divine!*

SERVES 4

4 tbsp sunflower or vegetable oil

A medium-sized free-range chicken, jointed into 8 pieces (or 8 pieces of your favourite cut)

Half a dozen garlic cloves, peeled and chopped

3cm piece of ginger, peeled and finely chopped

260ml water

1 fresh green chilli, deseeded and finely chopped

¼ tsp cayenne pepper

2 tsp ground cumin

1 tsp ground coriander

½ tsp ground turmeric

200g fresh coriander, finely chopped

Juice and zest of 1 lemon

Sea salt

In a heavy-bottomed pan, heat your oil and fry the chicken pieces until nicely coloured. They don't need to be cooked all the way through at this stage. Remove the chicken with a slotted spoon, and set to one side. Add the garlic and ginger to the oil and continue cooking for about 30 seconds before adding 60ml of the water.

Stir together and then add the chilli, cayenne pepper, cumin, ground coriander and turmeric, cooking for another 60 seconds before returning the chicken to the pan.

Add the remaining 200ml of water, a little sea salt to taste, the fresh coriander, and the juice and zest of the lemon. Stir through and simmer for 20 minutes. Serve immediately.

Spiced Rice

To make spiced rice, simply boil your rice with a piece of cinnamon, 3 cloves, 3 green cardamom pods and some salt and pepper. Remove the whole spices before serving. A knob of butter fluffed into the rice always works well too!

LAMB & POTATO CURRY (ALOO GOSHT)

Throughout the North we are blessed with a large Asian community who cook in cafés and restaurants all across the region and serve up delicious dishes quite different from our own. Most cook in an *appna* style, which means 'our way', and I love nothing better than a traditional *appna* curry with a couple of roti or chapatti at lunchtime. No knives or forks required – just bread. It's truly heaven! This is my kind of food and it beats a reheated pasty or a soulless sandwich hands down. These curries are very simple to eat *and* make and they use inexpensive, everyday ingredients.

SERVES 6

4 tbsp vegetable oil

280g onions, peeled and roughly chopped

2 fresh green chillies, halved and deseeded

7 garlic cloves, peeled and finely chopped

1kg lamb shoulder on the bone, cut into 2–3cm cubes (purchase from your local halal shop if you can)

400g tin of chopped tomatoes

2 tbsp masala powder, also known as basar (or garam masala if you can't find masala)

2 tsp sea salt

10 fresh curry leaves

1kg potatoes, peeled and cut into quarters (or halves, if small)

1.2 litres boiling water

2 whole black cardamom (available in Asian supermarkets)

A handful of finely chopped fresh coriander (optional)

In a large heavy-bottomed curry pan, heat the vegetable oil, adding the onion, chillies and garlic when hot. Let them cook for 5 minutes, stirring frequently, until lightly browned, and then throw in the meat (and the bones). Turn the heat down slightly and continue stirring for another 5 minutes.

Next, add your tin of tomatoes, the garam masala and the salt and stir to combine. Over medium heat, cook the ingredients until a shiny, oily sheen appears. Throw in your curry leaves, potato, boiling water and black cardamom and bring to a nice, slow simmer. Cook for about 60 minutes or until the potato starts to drop and thicken the sauce. Finish off with the finely chopped fresh coriander if using and a little more salt, to taste.

If possible, leave the curry to cool for a couple of hours to encourage the flavours to deepen. Reheat thoroughly before serving with spiced rice (see page 130) or chapatti.

ROASTS & PECULIARLY NORTHERN MEATS

Bringing a whole roast meat to the dinner table is a grand gesture. It's generous, civilised and celebratory, and there can be nothing quite as fulfilling as getting the family together at the weekend to enjoy a succulent roast dinner and share a bottle of wine or two. It gets us back to basics: we catch up with loved ones and mark the end of the working week, all around a centrepiece of glorious meat and veg. And lots of Northern kids loved 'bread and scrape': a doorstep of homemade white bread, liberally spread with the salty fat flecked with bits of brown crackling 'scraped' from the bottom of the Sunday roast tin. Never did me any harm. It's starting to reappear in trendy pubs and as ironic canapés in cool eateries up and down the country.

The custom of roast dinners dates back to the Industrial Revolution. Families would pop their meat into the oven and visit church or chapel for morning prayers. They'd follow this with a walk and arrive back for what we now call 'Sunday lunch'. Roasts were easy meals to prepare, and needed little tending once the meat hit the oven. Parents were freed from kitchen duties to spend time with the family, while the meat cooked itself. And there is something celebratory about a glistening joint placed in front of the whole family. It's an act that has serious pedigree. For centuries, our hunter-gatherer ancestors have been roasting meat on spits made of forged iron and other metals, creating feasts that tasted faintly of charred coals and smoky wood – delicious, juicy, nutritious and filling. The Vikings roasted a whole carcass in celebration of everything from battles to births, and tribes would meet to enjoy the meaty festivities with the same fervour that we enjoy our roasts today, and for exactly the same reasons.

With high cooking temperatures in our modern ovens, the process of creating a roast is more manageable and efficient, and we have a huge range of types and quality of meats to choose from. At the budget end of the market, we have what we would call 'wet' meat – young, fleshy joints with a high water content, which serves us well for an inexpensive family meal. And then, dear gastronauts, there are 'dry' hung meats, which have been aged a little to relax the muscles and tissues and relinquish a lot of the excess water in a cooled, controlled environment. This is softer, more elastic meat, and undoubtedly the more tender, sweeter option. Hung meat is pricier but tastier. Simple!

Creating a relationship with your butcher is one of the small pleasures in life and the reason for this is quite obvious. He or she knows the provenance of his or her meat, can tell you exactly how long it has been hung, and can point you in the direction of interesting and unusual cuts. He or she can prepare any cut of meat, to your specifications and for very special occasions. With enough notice, a good butcher will also source less familiar meats and offal that are particular to the North. Yes, the offal truth. Don't all groan at once! Until you've tried them, you won't know what you're missing. Some of our more delicious specialities include lamb's hearts (see page 147), black pudding, brawn (a jellied mould made from a pig's head, without the brain), chitterling (the small intestine of a pig), pigs' cheeks and trotters, cowheel (as it sounds – a cow's foot), elder (a cow's udder), haslet (a meatloaf of pork offal, lard, onions and caul – the fat from internal organs), oxtail and ox cheeks and tripe (the stomach lining of ruminant animals – see my recipe on page 149). These parts of the animal that other butchers might discard or chuck into their mince or burgers have a great flavour and texture, they're good sources of protein, and they're cheap. Our local butcher in Ashton Market sells a whole pig's head for £2.50!

There are lots of less familiar meats with which you can create something spectacular and different for literally pennies a head, so get to know the man or woman in the white apron, with the rotund belly and the pink cheeks, and use his or her experience to provide your family and friends with perfect cuts of meat.

Buying your special-offer 'wet' meat down at the supermarket may look like a bargain – and I know that in these times of austerity every penny counts –but we suggest that instead of buying two or three supermarket cuts every week, you go for one piece of fine-quality, farm-assured meat that won't shrink when you cook it, and will give you something truly special to enjoy. It's just a question of changing habits. And when you get to know your local butcher, you'll find that there are marvellous and inexpensive cuts of meat available that you'll simply never see on supermarket shelves. Up here in the North, we're good at saving money and that's why so many of our recipes use cuts and parts that other chefs ignore! Make your butcher your first port of call, and you'll glow with satisfaction when you taste the difference. Love me tender, indeed!

POT-ROAST BEEF

Of all the recipes in this book – all the vegetables, all the cuts of meat, all the puddings – this one takes the brisket! This is so simple and so tasty we dare you not to try it. Warning: The smells in your kitchen may be overwhelming, so keep a reviving glass of wine and a chair nearby. This is delicious served hot in a deep white bowl with mashed potato and the luscious thin gravy poured over the top. It's equally fantastic cold on an Oven-Bottom Muffin (see page 38), sprinkled generously with sea salt and, of course, a dollop of good English mustard.

SERVES 4

3 tbsp groundnut oil

1.25kg beef brisket

1 large onion, peeled and finely chopped

2 garlic cloves, peeled and chopped

2 turnips, peeled and quartered

2 celery stalks, chopped

2 carrots, peeled and quartered

1 star anise

Bouquet garni made from 1 celery stalk and 1 sprig each of fresh rosemary, sage and thyme, all tied together

1 large glass of red wine (plus some for sipping)

Sea salt and freshly ground black pepper

In a large, lidded stockpot, heat your groundnut oil and lovingly brown the brisket on all sides. Remove the beef onto a plate and set aside. Chuck in your onion, garlic, turnip, celery and carrot and cook over medium heat for 5 minutes. Add your star anise, bouquet garni and wine, and season to taste. Add enough hot water to cover the vegetables and return your brisket to the centre of the pot.

Bring to the boil, cover and simmer on the lowest heat for 3 hours. If you prefer, you can do it in the oven (covered) at 150°C/300°F/Gas mark 2 for 3 hours or in a slow cooker for up to 6 hours.

Slice the brisket, ladle the veggie broth over the meat and enjoy.

Without doubt, this is simple, braised, rustic, earthy cooking at its absolute finest! It's one of the best recipes in this book.

SALT BEEF

Salt Beef is a Jewish staple that I first tasted in a Jewish deli/café in Prestwich, Manchester. I had it piled on a bagel with pickled gherkins and was blown away by the tenderness of the meat and its astonishing flavour. And whilst any good salt beef counter is a mountain of meat, for a special occasion this is definitely worth trying at home. It's a bit of a meaty mammoth adventure, but go on, try a little tenderness!

SERVES AN ARMY!

4 litres water

620g coarse sea salt

350g Demerara sugar

4 bay leaves

2–3 sprigs of fresh thyme

1 tbsp black peppercorns, crushed

1 tbsp whole coriander seeds

10 whole allspice

1 free-range egg, in its shell

2.5kg beef brisket, trimmed of excess fat

1 garlic head, halved

Put the water, salt, sugar, herbs and spices in a large pan and bring to the boil. Remove from the heat and allow to cool. What you have now is a 'brine'. You want it really salty, so to check that, place the egg, still in its shell, into the brine; if it floats, the brine is salty enough. If it's not, add some more salt until the egg rises to the surface.

Once the brine has completely cooled, place your meat in a large plastic container with a lid. Add the garlic and pour over the brine. Because of the salt in the cure, the meat will float to the top. Place a heavy object on top of the meat to weigh it down and keep it fully submerged, then seal with the lid.

Write the date on a sticky label on top of your container, then put it into the fridge where it should be left to cure for a minimum of 5 days (for a lighter, less salty cure) or up to 2 weeks (for a more mature, rounded flavour). Over this time, you'll need to remove the container once a day to turn the meat, which ensures the cure is even. Reseal carefully after turning and don't forget to return it to the fridge.

When it's cured to your liking, tip the meat into a colander and wash it thoroughly for a few minutes to remove excess salt. Place in a large pan and cover with water. Bring to a simmer over a medium-high heat and skim off any impurities that float to the top. Cover and simmer for 3 to 4 hours, or until the meat is tender. Top up with water, if necessary. The brisket should be nicely covered throughout.

When it's cooked, carefully remove the beef and place it on a tray. Don't worry if it breaks up, that simply means that it's really tender. Salt beef can be served hot or cold. If you want yours hot, allow it to rest for a few minutes before slicing. Otherwise, place it in the fridge overnight, which makes it easier to slice.

POTTED BEEF

I've seen loads of recipes for Potted Beef over the years, but my favourite is this lovely beefy, stringy, cold and satisfying version that Simon Hopkinson discovered when Glenys K. Pople from Stockport in Cheshire sent him the recipe. Simon published it in his book *Gammon and Spinach* and this is by far the best! It must, of course, be eaten smeared on warm toast with a glass of beer and pickles.

SERVES 4-6

1kg lower shin beef (this cut makes the perfect Potted Beef)

Sea salt and freshly ground black pepper

Cut off the fat and any sinewy bits from the beef, but leave as much of the internal marbling as possible. Cut the beef into fingernail-sized cubes. Place in a saucepan and cover with water. Bring to the boil and keep it on the boil for about 10–15 minutes, skimming until no froth remains.

Cover and simmer very gently, adding water from time to time to keep the beef covered. After 3 or 4 hours, when the meat separates into individual fibres (or 'goes to rags'), turn up the heat and boil hard to get rid of the water, stirring the mixture vigorously with a fork to break up the meat. When the beef is moist, but not wet, remove from the heat and season generously with sea salt and pepper.

Potted Beef is eaten cold, and therefore more seasoning than usual will be required. Pile into an old-fashioned pudding bowl, pack down well, and then place a saucer on the top. Weight it down with a tin of beans (or the like) and refrigerate for at least 24 hours. Remove the saucer and then invert the pudding bowl onto a plate and serve the Potted Beef. Easy peasy lemon squeezy!

Baked to crisp perfection,
a Northern Yorkshire
pudding isn't just a
Sunday staple – it's
culinary genius!

YORKIES FROM HEAVEN

From where heralds the sublime Yorkshire pudding? What genius first came up with the idea of combining flour with fat to make delicious little batter puddings that can cook in the oven with the Sunday roast? They'd probably been around for ages by the time a recipe first appeared in print, in a 1737 book controversially named *The Whole Duty of a Woman*. In there they were referred to as 'dripping puddings', because the idea was that they sat beneath your roast to catch the drippings.

A decade later, pioneering Northumberland cookery writer Hannah Glasse mentioned them in her 1747 cookbook *The Art of Cookery Made Plain and Easy*, and it was she who first called them Yorkshire puds in print (although they must have been known to Yorkshire folks as such for ages before that). In those days they were often served before the meal to fill an empty tummy before the more expensive meat came along.

Then a century later, Southerner Mrs Beeton mentioned them in her classic *Mrs Beeton's Cookbook*, but got the recipe wrong because she didn't mention that you need a really hot oven! Hers must have been really soggy and horrible...

However you want to make your puds – individually or in one large tray – there are a few pointers that will help to make the process foolproof.

Ingredients should be at room temperature before you embark on the recipe.

Always, always rest your batter before cooking. Some Northerners keep it refrigerated overnight. This may be a little extreme, but resting does make the batter lighter.

Avoid over-filling the tin; one-third full is usually sufficient.

Never use butter or olive oil. They will burn past a certain temperature and never get hot enough anyhow.

Make sure your fat is *smokin'* before you even think about filling the tins, and get that batter in there as quickly as you can.

Avoid opening the oven while cooking; the rush of air can make the puds collapse.

Don't wash your Yorkshire pudding tin with detergent, as this can spoil the surface of the tin and prevent your puddings from rising. Simply wipe clean with kitchen paper after use.

Serve them straight from the oven; nothing worse than a deflated Yorkshire pudding (or family).

THE PERFECT YORKSHIRE PUD

The Royal Society of Chemistry tells us that, 'A Yorkshire Pudding is a combination of carbohydrate + H2O + protein + NaCl + lipids'. OK, er, thank you boys. In my book, a perfect Yorkshire is something pretty special: hot, light, crisp and as fresh as fresh can be – straight out of the oven, covered with a lovely, thick brown gravy and straight out to your family, guests or significant other! This recipe creates the perfect Yorkshire Pudding every time – guaranteed. And not a scientific equation in sight!

SERVES 6

4 large free-range eggs
Equal quantity of milk to eggs
Pinch of salt
Equal quantity of flour to eggs
Lard, beef dripping or
    vegetable oil

Preheat the oven to 230°C/450°F/Gas mark 9.

Pour the eggs into a measuring jug (choose one that's a good pourer). This is how you'll judge that you've got equal amounts. Add an equal amount of milk and whisk thoroughly until you have a smooth batter, then add a pinch of salt. Leave to stand for about 10 minutes.

Next, sieve an equal amount of flour into the egg and milk and whisk again to create a lump-free batter. Pass the batter through a sieve into a bowl and leave it to rest for at least 30 minutes (the longer the better).

In the oven, preheat a baking tin with twelve small indentations or six large ones. Take it out and place a pea-sized piece of lard or dripping or ½ teaspoon vegetable oil into each indentation. Heat in the oven until the fat is smoking. Give the batter another good whisk, adding 2 tsp water.

Remove the tin from the oven (be sure to use gloves!) and quickly fill one-third of each indentation. Return to the oven and cook until the puddings are well risen and golden brown (approximately 12–15 minutes). Serve as a starter with hot gravy or as part of your menu for the Sunday roast.

LIVER 'N' ONIONS

Comfort food at its best, this hearty combination of thinly sliced lamb's liver with a sweet, sticky, sumptuous, bubbling gravy is a Great Northern staple. Liver remains a nutritious and inexpensive ingredient, and it never fails to deliver a hefty Northern punch that provides the basis for a perfect midweek winter warmer. Easy and cheap to prepare, and as lush as 'oot', this is a dish you simply have to try.

SERVES 4

70g flour

4 portions of lamb's liver, about 170g each

2–3 tbsp groundnut oil

1 large onion, peeled, halved and then thinly sliced

300ml beef stock, plus a little extra

8 small turnips, peeled and cut into 2cm pieces

3–4 dashes of Worcestershire sauce

1 glass of red wine

Sea salt and ground white pepper

Preheat the oven to 180°C/350°F/Gas mark 4.

Season your flour with salt and pepper, place in a large bowl and liberally coat each piece of liver. Next, in a good-sized frying pan, heat your groundnut oil till sizzling and quickly brown the liver on both sides. Remove the liver with a slotted spoon and add the onion to the pan, scraping up any of the bits of browned liver and flour that remain. Cook the onion for 3 minutes, then stir in 100ml of your beef stock and tip the contents of the pan into your favourite large casserole dish.

Add your liver, the remaining beef stock, turnips, Worcestershire sauce and red wine, and season with salt and white pepper. Stir to combine, cover and place in the middle of your oven. Cook for about 60 minutes, or until bubbling and fragrant.

Once it's cooked, remove from the oven and gently stir and taste for seasoning. We like to eat this with mashed potato and swede – equal portions of potatoes and swede mashed together with butter, milk, sea salt and white pepper. Place your mash in the centre of a large bowl, lay on a piece of the liver, and carefully and lovingly smother with this outrageously delicious gravy. Enjoy!

STUFFED LAMB'S HEARTS WITH CELERIAC MASH

There's no reason to be squeamish! Just go to the butcher, take a deep breath and confidently ask for four lamb's hearts. It's as easy as that, and you'll be well rewarded for your efforts. Heart is, and always has been, a great Northern meal and a staple for many with a family to feed on a budget. Heart is full of protein and has a gorgeous flavour that you won't fail to appreciate once you've tasted it. Accompanied by my smooth, creamy Celeriac Mash and smothered in rich gravy, you'll have a dish that is, quite simply, unrivalled.

SERVES 4

For the celeriac mash

4 King Edward potatoes, peeled and quartered

½ celeriac, peeled and chopped into 2.5cm cubes

2 tsp salted butter

100ml full-fat milk (you might need a bit more with floury potatoes, less with waxy)

Sea salt and ground white pepper

For the lamb's hearts

1 tbsp beef dripping or butter

3 red onions, peeled and finely chopped

8 garlic cloves, peeled and chopped

1 large glass of red wine

220g stale white bread, crusts off and cubed

10 fresh sage leaves, chopped

4 lamb's hearts

8 rashers of streaky bacon

1 litre chicken stock

Sea salt and ground white pepper

In a large saucepan, cover your potato and celeriac with water and bring to the boil. Reduce the heat and simmer until tender. Drain and return to the pan. Add the butter and cover to let the butter melt. Take off the lid and mash, slowly adding milk to create a creamy consistency. Season and cover.

To make the lamb's hearts, melt your dripping or butter in a frying pan and add your onion and garlic. Cook gently until translucent, but not coloured. Add the wine and cook until it is reduced by half, then add your bread, a little at a time, to create an unctuous mixture. Season. Continue cooking for 15 minutes. Cool slightly and stir in the sage leaves.

Preheat the oven to 180°C/350°F/Gas mark 4. Trim the hearts, removing any fatty nodules and sinews so that the flap at the top of the heart can be used to cover the opening later on. Next, use your fingers to scoop out any blood clots at the base of the ventricles. You could ask your butcher to do this.

Press the oniony stuffing into each heart until the chambers are filled right to the top, then bring the flap down to cover the stuffing. Use two rashers of bacon for each heart and form a cross over the top opening to secure. Stand the hearts upright in a deep roasting tray and pour stock around them. Cover with foil and scrunch it down around the edges of the tray to secure. Cook for 2½ hours.

Remove from the oven and lift out the hearts onto a warm serving dish. Stir any stuffing that has escaped into the juices and season to taste. Serve the hearts on top of the mash, and smother with gravy.

DEEP-FRIED TRIPE

Tripe grows in the swampy mangroves of Bolton and only flourishes on a Wednesday (market day). Albert Eccleshall, legendary clog maker and part-time tripe gatherer, says, 'There's only one way to eat tripe and that's deep fried in beer batter. Once bitten, tripe shy!'

SERVES LOTS

250g plain flour, plus 4 tbsp for coating

60g cornflour

250ml lager (freezing cold)

250ml soda water (freezing cold)

A mixture of white, black and cayenne peppers to make up 1 level tsp

Vegetable oil, for deep-frying

450g sheet of honeycomb tripe

To make the beer batter, sift the flour and cornflour in a large bowl and whisk together. Add the beer and soda water and mix to incorporate, then whisk vigorously to get rid of any lumps. Let stand for 10 minutes and then whisk again for 30 seconds. If for some reason there are still lumps, simply strain them out. The batter will fry crispier if not refrigerated. Now add your peppers and whisk through.

Heat up vegetable oil for deep-frying in a suitable pan. Check if it's hot enough by dropping in a piece of bread and if it sizzles, it's ready.

For the tripe, cut your tripe into whatever shape suits you for a goujon size. Season the flour in a bowl with salt and pepper, then douse each goujon liberally with the seasoned flour.

Now, dip each goujon into the batter and drop carefully into the hot oil. Once floating and golden brown, the goujons are done. Carefully, with a slotted spoon, drop onto kitchen roll to drain before serving to the minions. Tripetastic!

THE BARNSLEY CHOP

This may sound like a defensive move you'd need outside a club on a Saturday night, like our equivalent of the Glaswegian kiss, but in fact it is a special kind of lamb chop cut from the centre of the loin across both sides of the saddle, giving it a butterfly shape. Various establishments claim to have invented the Barnsley chop, but after a lot of research food critic Matthew Fort concluded that it originated at the King's Head Hotel on Market Hill, Barnsley in 1849 – and who are we to argue? (Although the Brooklands Hotel in Barnsley also claims credit.)

These monster chops – weighing around 600g each – were served to wealthy farmers on market day and you could only get two from each sheep. They were dressed and hung for ten days to make sure they were tender, and served with chips and a local Barnsley beer.

Now, I've yet to find a supermarket that sells Barnsley chops, so you'll need to befriend your local butcher to get your paws on some. And purists will say they should only come from sheep reared on the moors and dales of Yorkshire. Whaddever!

Cook the chops by seasoning with salt and pepper, then either frying in a little oil or grilling under a preheated grill for 8–10 minutes, turning halfway through. Exact timing depends on the thickness of the meat, but they should be brown on the outside and pink in the middle, without actually bleeding onto the plate.

Lamb is traditionally served with mint sauce, a habit that goes back to the days when mutton was more common than it is now. Mutton is meat from sheep more than a year old, and has a strong, gamey flavour and smell, which mint helps to mask. Lamb comes from sheep aged four months to a year and is more tender. Personally I like to serve chops with a simple redcurrant sauce made by boiling up 4 tablespoons redcurrant jelly with a glass of port and reducing to thicken slightly. If you prefer mint sauce, make your own by combining a handful of fresh mint leaves, 4 tablespoons white wine vinegar, 1 tablespoon caster sugar, 4 tablespoons boiling water and a pinch of salt.

I'm not a Yorkshireman myself, but they like their Barnsley chops and, as you probably know, a Yorkshireman is always bloody well right.

PORK BELLY WITH BAKED BEANS

Pork belly is traditional Northern grub, and we've put together this recipe to give it all the Northern twists we can. The homemade baked beans recipe is from the brilliant Lancashire chef Paul Heathcote – thanks, mate! They're rich and smooth, just perfect accompanied by the crisp exterior of the pork, with its mouth-watering softly textured meaty centre, and the silky bay leaf sauce. Don't forget to pile it all on a creamy base of buttered mashed potatoes.

SERVES 4

For the baked beans

2 x 400g tins of haricot beans

1 onion, peeled and chopped

1 sprig of fresh thyme

900ml chicken stock

For the bay leaf sauce

8 shallots, peeled and finely chopped

2 garlic cloves, peeled and finely chopped

5 bay leaves

1 knob of salted butter

100ml port

100ml Madeira wine

500ml red wine

250ml brown chicken stock (see page 62)

For the pork belly

1 tbsp groundnut oil

1 shallot, peeled and chopped

3 garlic cloves, peeled and chopped

2 sprigs of fresh rosemary

2.5cm-thick slices of pork belly (about 250g each)

1 can of cider (500ml)

1 tbsp Worcestershire sauce

Buttered mashed potato, to serve

Drain the beans and place them in a saucepan with the onion, thyme and chicken stock. Bring to the boil, and then turn off the heat, cover, and put to one side to infuse.

Preheat the oven to 180°C/350°F/Gas mark 4.

Sweat the shallot, garlic and bay leaves in butter over a gentle heat for 10 minutes until the shallot and garlic have turned nicely golden. Add the port and Madeira wine and continue cooking until the liquid has reduced by about two-thirds. Add the red wine and cook until it has reduced by half. Stir in the chicken stock and bring to the boil. Cook for about 5 minutes until you have a thick sauce that coats the back of a spoon, skimming and stirring as it cooks. Sieve and put to one side.

In a frying pan, heat the groundnut oil for the pork belly and add the shallot, garlic and rosemary. Cook over a gentle heat for about 5 minutes or until the shallot begins to 'sweat'. Place the pork belly in a deep roasting tray or dish and cover with the onion and garlic. Pour over the can of cider and the Worcestershire sauce and place on the top shelf of the oven. Roast for 40–50 minutes or until golden and crispy.

Rustle up your very best mashed potatoes, reheat your beans and sauce, and carve your pork belly into four servings. Place the pork belly on top of the mashed potato, sieve your beans, mix them into the bay leaf sauce and arrange them around the plate.

Great Northern food at its finest!

PORK CRACKLING

There is nothing – simply nothing – that can beat Crackling with your Roast Pork at Sunday lunch. There is something rather carnal about rubbing the oil into the skin...oh, Matron! On the other hand, there is nothing worse than Pork Crackling with the fat sitting beneath the skin, so give your butcher your biggest smile and ask him to remove the soft fat from beneath. Do this and you will have the perfect Crackling every time!

Pork rind, preferably from the loin

Groundnut oil or lard

Sea salt

Preheat the oven to 200°C/400°/Gas mark 6.

Take your sharpest knife and score the skin in a crisscross fashion, being careful not to go all the way through the skin. Using your fingers, take your oil or lard and rub thoroughly all over and into the skin.

Now, take a good handful of sea salt and rub this all over the oiled skin.

Place in the oven for 30–40 minutes, until the rind becomes nice and crunchy.

RACK OF RIBS 'N' CABBAGE

The North has always had a great affinity with the Irish – not to mention Irish-style cooking – and this dish ticks all the boxes. The very simple mix of hammy ribs and sweet, buttery cabbage will light your fire! The smells around your kitchen will whet the appetite of your guests like never before and there will be 'nowt' left on the plate...that's a guarantee!

SERVES 4

1 rack of 12 pork ribs, cut in half (by your friendly butcher)

1 white cabbage, halved and coarsely sliced

Sea salt and ground white pepper

Lashings of real butter

Place your pork ribs in a stockpot and liberally cover with water. Bring to the boil and skim as necessary. Reduce the heat, cover and then simmer for 30 minutes. Remove the ribs and wrap in foil to keep them warm.

Add your cabbage to the same water and simmer, uncovered, for 30 minutes. Drain and season with salt and pepper. Divide onto four plates and top with lashings of butter. Carve the ribs into four servings and place on top of the cabbage.

Now, rip apart the ribs and suck them dry while forking in mounds of delicious, buttery cabbage. Reet gradely!

PIG IN A GINNEL

Up North, if you see a bowlegged man walking down the street you say, 'He wouldn't stop a pig in a ginnel.' A ginnel is a passageway between two houses that allows access to the backyard and a man with bow legs couldn't stop a pig in one because it would run straight through his legs. Pig in a Ginnel is my name for a flaky, savoury, piping-hot delight of a sausage roll.

SERVES AT LEAST 4

400g raw ham shoulder

200g pork shoulder

200g smoked back bacon, untrimmed

(Ask your butcher to put all the meats through his mincer twice; if you've bought the meat ingredients from a supermarket, whizz them all thoroughly in a food processor)

8 shallots, peeled and finely chopped

1–2 tbsp mustard powder

3 tbsp honey

2 tsp ground white pepper

1kg block of puff pastry (shop bought is fine)

2 free-range eggs, beaten

A squirt of honey

A pinch of mustard powder

Parmesan cheese, finely grated

Silverskin onions, to serve

Preheat the oven to 200°C/400°F/Gas mark 6.

Place the meats in a large mixing bowl and add the shallot, mustard, honey and white pepper. Mix all the ingredients thoroughly. Wrap your meat mixture in cling film and chill for an hour. On a lightly floured surface, roll out the pastry into a rectangle just over A4 size, with one of the shorter sides facing you.

Take the meat mixture out of the fridge. Tear off a tennis-ball-sized piece and manipulate into a rough sausage shape. Lay it on the work surface and roll into a neat sausage that's as long as the shorter edge of the pastry. It should be around 3cm thick. Place the sausage on the pastry, 3cm in from the edge nearest you. Lift the edge and with flat hands slowly roll the pastry around the sausage.

When it reaches the pastry on the other side, brush an area of about 3cm with the beaten egg. Lightly score the egged area with a knife, but be careful not to pierce it. Continue your 'roll' over the egged area to join the puff pastry edges together. Run a knife down the length of the roll to cut off the rest of the pastry.

Now turn the sausage roll so that the joined edge is upwards. Neaten up the join and make sure you have a good seal, then turn it join side down and place it on a greased baking tray. Make another three rolls and place on the same baking tray, but make sure they are comfortably apart from each other.

Mix the remaining beaten egg with a squirt of honey and the pinch of mustard. Paint the rolls generously with your egg wash. Sprinkle with Parmesan cheese, then bake for 20 minutes, until golden brown and puffed up. Take out of the oven and cut each of the rolls into three. Plate up three hot rolls per person, accompanied by cold silverskin onions.

BOILED HAM WITH PARSLEY HOLLANDAISE SAUCE

According to Andrew Webb, author of foodie bible *Food Britannia*, York ham was created in the mid-nineteenth century by a man called Robert Burrow Atkinson. He had a butcher's shop in Blossom Street, York, with a cellar that was perfect for maturing hams. Customers flocked to buy his produce and York ham was 'born'. This is my take on the classic.

SERVES 4

2kg bacon collar, boned, skinned, rolled and tied

1 large onion, peeled and roughly chopped

2 carrots, peeled and roughly chopped

2 celery stalks, roughly chopped

2 bay leaves

For the hollandaise

6 crushed black peppercorns

1 tbsp white wine vinegar

2 free-range egg yolks

200g butter, melted

Sea salt

3–4 drops of lemon juice

Fresh parsley, finely chopped

The day before you plan to cook and/or serve your ham, soak the bacon collar in cold, fresh water and leave overnight. This releases any excess salt to provide a better taste. Once soaked, wash the collar and place in a large saucepan or soup pan with all of the vegetables and your bay leaves and cover with water. Put a lid on, bring to a simmer and cook for 60–90 minutes, skimming regularly. Remove your bacon from the water and leave to rest for 30 minutes.

While it's resting, make your hollandaise. Place the peppercorns and vinegar in a stainless steel saucepan and bring to the boil. Reduce by one third, and then remove from the heat. Stir in 1 tablespoon of water and allow to cool. Take out the peppercorns.

Whisk in your egg yolks and return to a gentle heat, whisking continuously until your sauce has thickened. A creamy consistency that leaves the mark of the whisk is just right. Now, gradually whisk in your warm, melted butter until thoroughly combined. Taste for seasoning and add a few drops of lemon juice.

Pass the sauce through a sieve and stir in the parsley. Keep warm until ready to serve.

Carve your bacon collar into nice thick slices and serve on warm plates, smothered with the hollandaise sauce. A side of well-peppered, cracked new potatoes and white cabbage will complete this dish to perfection. And if you have anything left over the following day, your ham and hollandaise sauce will make a sublime Eggs Benedict!

HAM HOCK TERRINE

There is nothing nicer than visiting summer markets to pick up the ingredients for this savoury terrine – a perfect lunchtime dish, to be served with fresh mustard, silverskin onions, pickled gherkins and a flagon of good, robust cider. I use my sharpest, most impressive carving knife to expertly slice the terrine for my friends and family. Summer eating at its best! Do note that you'll need to start preparing this dish a couple of days before you plan to eat it.

SERVES 4–5

2 x 1kg ham hocks (more than you'll need, but save the rest for sandwiches)

1 large onion, peeled and roughly chopped

2 carrots, peeled and roughly chopped

2 turnips, peeled and roughly chopped

2 sprigs of fresh rosemary

2 sprigs of fresh thyme

10 black peppercorns

½ bulb fennel

1 tbsp cider vinegar

2.5 litres water

2 gelatine leaves

1 large bunch of fresh parsley, finely chopped

1 large bunch of large-leaf spinach, spines removed

Sea salt (just a little) and freshly ground black pepper

Soak your ham hocks overnight in two changes of fresh water.

Place the ham in a large pan, cover with fresh water and bring to the boil, skimming frequently. Add the vegetables, rosemary, thyme, peppercorns, fennel and vinegar. Simmer for 2 hours, until the ham is falling off the bone.

Take out the hocks, strip the meat from the bone and place in a mixing bowl. Add the parsley to the ham and season. Sieve ½ litre of the vegetable liquor into a measuring jug and discard the vegetables. Soften the gelatine in a pint glass of cold water for 2 minutes, then add to the vegetable liquor, stirring well.

Bring a pan with 1 litre of water up to a simmer, then blanch your spinach leaves for 1 minute. Refresh them in cold water. Dry the leaves thoroughly.

Lightly grease a 1lb loaf tin with vegetable oil and line it with cling film, overlapping by 8cm either side. Lightly grease the inside of the cling film, then lay the spinach leaves around it, overlapping 8cm at the top to match the cling film.

Spoon the ham and parsley into the loaf tin. Pour over enough of the gelatine liquid to just cover the ham. Fold the spinach leaves and cling film over the top to cover. Place another loaf tin on top of your terrine and put two tins of beans inside to weigh it down. Chill for 12 hours, until set.

Turn your terrine out onto a chopping board, unpeel the cling film and slice into the terrine. Serve with cornichons and crusty bread.

MEATLOAF WITH CARAMELISED ONIONS

Meatloaf, or 'Dead Man's Leg' as we used to call it as kids, is a great Northern treat and brings back vivid memories of the lip-smacking teatimes of my childhood. Served with fluffy mash and smothered in lashings of gravy, this is a quick, scrumptious dish for the whole family. Be generous with the gravy, 'cos Northerners just love the stuff!

SERVES 4

For the meatloaf

500g minced beef

500g minced pork

4 onions, peeled and finely chopped

1 carrot, finely chopped

2 free-range eggs

100g stale white breadcrumbs (no crusts)

1 tsp sea salt

½ tsp freshly ground black pepper

2 tbsp fresh sage, finely chopped

2 tbsp fresh parsley

1 tbsp good English mustard

1 tbsp Worcestershire sauce or Henderson's Relish

2–3 dashes of chilli sauce

For the caramelised onions

2 tbsp vegetable oil

2 large onions, peeled and thinly sliced

Sea salt

To serve

Buttered mashed potato

The Perfect Gravy (page 206)

Preheat the oven to 180°C/350°F/Gas mark 4.

In a large mixing bowl, combine the beef and pork mince, onion, carrot, eggs, breadcrumbs, salt, pepper, sage, half the parsley, mustard, Worcestershire sauce and chilli sauce. Mix together – go on get your hands in there! Once perfectly combined, press into a large loaf tin lined with baking paper or form a loaf with your hands and place on a baking tray. Sprinkle with the remaining parsley. Bake for about 60 minutes, or until the juices run clear when the loaf is pierced.

Meanwhile, to make the caramelised onions, heat your vegetable oil in a heavy-bottomed pan and add the onions, sautéeing for approximately 20 minutes over a medium heat. Add a pinch of salt as you cook and this will help them turn lovely and caramelly. Once cooked set aside.

Remove your meatloaf from the oven and let it rest for 10 minutes. Drain off any fat and then turn it out onto a platter. Slice and serve on top of fluffy buttered mashed potato, covered in lovely, meaty gravy and topped with the caramelised onion.

Go on... try to convince
me that there is anything
better than homegrown
Northern English lamb...

FROM FIELD TO FORK

Jimmy 'The Lambman' Bell is a legend round here. With ten generations of farming behind him, he and his wife Kirsty run East Wingates Farm near Morpeth, Northumberland, bringing some of the finest lamb you'll ever taste. This is an enterprise run strictly to key dates: ewes are prepared for 'tupping' (mating) about 10 weeks before Jimmy's deadline of 5 November, when the nights become longer and the sheep come into season. The rams (tups) are pulled out on Christmas Eve, and the ewes are scanned on Valentine's Day, to see how many lambs they are carrying – no romance for some!

Pregnant ewes are given plenty of natural herbage with feed concentrates to get them in tip-top condition to carry their lambs to term and offer them plenty of highly nutritious milk once they are born. Around March, the ewes carrying singles, twins and triplets are separated, and those carrying multiples are brought into the sheds for a little extra attention. Come April (traditionally the school holidays, when extra hands would be available), lambing begins! This is intensive work, folks, with Jimmy delivering and tending to his new arrivals from 4am till 10pm every day, with Kirsty taking over the night shift, for at least six weeks. Alongside this, as the summer months draw near, sheep need to be clipped, hay brought in and rowdy crowds of sheep and lambs given simply the finest care.

In fact, Jimmy's determined to give his lambs the best possible start – milk on tap and then, when they are separated from the ewes, sweet, natural grass for grazing, fresh air, plenty of space to frolic, and a view like no other. This is just one reason why Northern lamb is so special: open skies, a diet of fragrant, juicy herbage and fresh water, and clean air fed by breezes off the North Sea. On a quiet Monday morning, the lambs are taken to the local slaughterhouse and their carcasses returned to Jimmy for butchering on the farm. He chills them for a week (two weeks for later in the season to naturally mature), and his customers know just when to turn up for the finest, most succulent lamb in the North.

Jimmy had a skill exchange with some Romanian butchers a few years back and has fine-tuned the art of smoking some of his lamb over beech, too. The rest he cuts into Barnsley chops, rolled shoulders, chops, leg joints – you name it. We're mad about lamb in the North, and grateful to farmers – custodians of the countryside – like Jimmy for giving us quality produce to make our hotpots, pies, Sunday roasts, curries, lamb sausages and even gluten-free lamb burgers.

GARLIC ROAST CHICKEN

Chicken and garlic – it's the perfect combination. Or should we say, garlic and chicken, because that's what makes this recipe so fantastic. The first time Rev and I tried this dish it blew us away – literally. We had heard that chewing on some parsley would eliminate the smell on our breath; however, not only did it not work, but the combination of garlic breath and green teeth didn't get us very far when chatting up the girls. So save this recipe for nights when you're not looking to pull.

SERVES 4

1 medium free-range chicken

2 lemons

6 whole garlic heads, halved, with the skin on

2 bay leaves

1 sprig of fresh thyme

50g best unsalted butter

3 tbsp sunflower oil

250ml glass of dry white wine

Splash of chicken stock made with a stock cube (optional)

Sea salt and freshly ground black pepper

A small pot (142ml) of single cream

Preheat the oven to 180°C/350°F/Gas mark 4. Rub the chicken inside and out with salt and pepper. Place it in a roasting tin or dish. Squeeze the lemons and pour the juice inside and over the chicken. Stuff the bird with three of your halved garlics, the bay leaves and the thyme. Stuff one of the squeezed lemons inside the chicken.

Remove five to six of the garlic cloves from the remaining garlic. With a knife, pierce the chicken skin. Stick the garlic cloves under the skin with some of the butter. Smear any remaining butter over the outside of the bird. Pour the sunflower oil over the chicken and pop your bird into the oven for about 30 minutes.

After this time remove from the oven, surround the chicken with the remaining unpeeled garlic and squeezed lemon. Baste the chicken and garlic with the pan juices. Return to the oven and cook for another 45 minutes, basting regularly until golden brown. To check, pierce it with a sharp knife. If the juices run clear, it's ready.

Remove the bird from the oven and place it onto a large serving dish. Spoon out the garlic and lemon that was inside the bird's cavity and put these back into the roasting dish together with the garlic and lemon from around the chicken.

Spoon off any excess oil in the roasting dish. Add the wine to the juices and heat through, stirring constantly. If you want, add chicken stock at this stage. Season and strain into a saucepan. From the strained bits, add any remaining garlic halves to the chicken on the serving dish. Finally, add the cream to the saucepan. Warm once more and pour over your chicken.

CHICKEN WITH BAY, GARLIC & WHITE WINE

Modern home chefs now demand fine ingredients and delicious, achievable recipes, and I've mustered up a chicken dish that ticks all the boxes! We Northerners simply love our one-pot meals and this is the modern equivalent because everything is thrown into a roasting tin and cooked together. Choose free-range chicken for finest results, and then slam this dish on the table in front of a load of friends and a glass or two of your favourite wines. Don't be afraid to use a roasting tin on your hob – just cook over two rings simultaneously! This is one of my favourite dishes.

SERVES 4

4 tbsp olive oil (not virgin)

2 garlic heads, cloves separated but skin on

1 medium free-range chicken, jointed into 8 pieces

6 bay leaves

300ml white wine

200ml water

Sea salt and freshly ground black pepper

Preheat the oven to 180°C/350°F/Gas mark 4.

Place a roasting tin on your hob and heat the olive oil to hot. Add the garlic cloves and fry gently until slightly golden. Remove with a slotted spoon and set to one side. Add your chicken pieces to the hot oil and fry until golden brown all over. Return the garlic to the pan and add the bay leaves. Pour in the white wine and then shake the pan to help the wine emulsify with the oil. Simmer for 2 minutes to evaporate the oil, and then stir in the water. Simmer for a further 4 minutes, and then place in the oven for 40 minutes.

Pierce your chicken with a sharp knife to check the juices run clear, then remove the bay leaves and season with salt and pepper. Serve in a large serving bowl in the middle of the table and invite your guests to pitch in and rip off bits with their fingers. Supply plenty of napkins!

BLACK BETTY, BAM-BA-LAM...

I'm pretty sure that all of you will have tried a slice of black pudding with a traditional English breakfast, and this is one Northern dish that is happily eaten by even the most squeamish of gourmets. The main ingredient is, of course, pork blood, with the careful addition of barley, oats, salt, white pepper, mustard, allspice and little cubes of pork fat. Once upon a time fresh pork blood was used, but because it has to be in constant motion to prevent coagulation – not ideal for today's busy marketplace – I reckon that dried blood has taken its place. This queen of breakfast puddings should be boiled and simmered, to keep the skin intact, but we will concede that grilling or frying it is an acceptable option!

We are absolutely blessed to have Bury Market up here in the North because when it comes to black pudding, there is no finer place to go. While researching this book, Rev and I visited the two main pudding-makers in Bury: Chadwick's and The Bury Black Pudding Company, both of whom claim to have the definitive recipe. These recipes have been passed down through generations and are fiercely guarded, and the friendly rivalry between them makes for a boisterous and lively atmosphere in one of the busiest markets in the North. And that's only one bit of black pud competition. The North is also host to the World Black Pudding Throwing Championships. If you can't eat it, chuck it!

Black pudding is cooked at the market in large vats of simmering water, and served in twists of greaseproof paper. There is always a range of good Northern condiments available to dollop onto the pudding: brown sauce, Piccalilli and even malt vinegar. Don't forget white pepper, too, to enliven the moist, luscious black interior. For the record, your pud is good if it's as black as a puppy dog's nose!

There can be nothing nicer than joining the throng of hungry black pudding addicts on a warm weekend morning, standing round the condiments table at the back of a stall and gnawing on these gems of Northernness. Which one's our favourite? There's not much between them, but we were won over by the pepperiness of Chadwick's recipe. You can buy them in most Northern butchers and markets, but if you're beholden to your local supermarket, make sure you get the stuff from the North. Better still, take a trip to the world-famous, award-winning stalls on Bury Market and try the real thing for yourself. Only a quid will get you into the exclusive pudding club!

There's nowt as good as a good black pud — savoury, succulent heaven. We won't be having any of that fussy-eater nonsense round here, either.

VEGETABLES

I absolutely love, adore and idolise vegetables! During many long hours of research for this book (and over many glasses of my favourite red wines), I only went and found out that vegetarianism was *founded in Salford!* Back in 1807, the unfortunately named Reverend William Cowherd formed a movement within his congregation to renounce the intake of meat. He is reported to have said that if God had meant us to eat meat, it would have come to us 'ready to eat' – like ripened fruit. OK, maybe that's dodgy logic and a tad overstated, but he appears to have been behind the birth of vegetarianism. Veggies have always been popular up here in the North and there's no doubt that we like to show them a little respect. For a boy from Manchester, it was enlightening to find out that an international movement shared my birthplace. I was even more fascinated to learn that in the 1880s there were more veggie restaurants in Manchester than there are today! You're twistin' ma melons, man!

Throughout my travels up and down the Great North, I have found the world of vegetables to be the most amazing of all. To me, veggies are just as important as any piece of pork, fillet of fish or silverside of beef. In fact, no great meal is complete without them. Rev and I met dozens of producers and many top chefs, such as Jean-Christophe Novelli, who adore vegetables as much as we do and we've learned to use them in a wide variety of ways. In the last twenty years, this country has seen a surge in the amazing quality and diversity of vegetables and fruit now available, and we are learning how to use them. Before the rise of the 'celebrity chef', veggies were pretty underrated. We had our overcooked, usually boiled, cauliflowers and carrots alongside soggy, drenched potatoes with little or no seasoning and, of course, a side of ubiquitous cabbage or peas. Beige, orange and green were the primary colours of the vegetable world, and they certainly did not inspire. Neither did the dreaded school dinner, which managed to boil out every nutrient and fibre from even the freshest veg. One of my favourite jokes from *Viz's Countdown to Christmas* is, 'November: time to put the sprouts on.'

Times have changed! Now we have a glorious array of vegetables available in a multitude of colours. We've even gone and brought back the purple carrot. And Yorkshire asparagus, from the area round Sand Hutton, is becoming much sought-after. We've learned to steam, stir-fry, blanch, braise and rinse to retain colour, texture, nutrition and, most of all, flavour. We've made vegetables a staple part of a healthy meal, on even the tightest budgets. If I had to choose one important addition to great British cooking over the last 30 years, it's the new respect for vegetables – a whole cornucopia of them!

In this book, I've tried to create as many veggie recipes as possible. But we do have to remember that we're all about Northern grub here, and we're ... er... not exactly renowned for our veggie options. We come from the land of black puddings and pork belly and we mush our dried peas rather than steam 'em fresh. But I have tried to include as many vegetables as possible in the meat dishes – to bring them bang up to date and convey my passionate belief that veggies are the business. Use them constantly and choose them with the care you would take at your favourite fishmonger or butcher. Making the effort to find fresh, seasonal produce, instead of wilting exotic ones with more air miles than Richard Branson, will pay dividends in the end.

Here in Manchester, we are lucky to have New Smithfield Market, which is a massive meeting ground for wholesale fruit and veg purveyors. They bring in tons and tons of fresh produce on a daily basis, and are instrumental in radiating it around the North. The premises are roughly the size of two Old Traffords and you almost need a guide to get round. Word of warning: if you are serious about your veg, you'll need to be there around 3am, as the real business is conducted before most of us have even wiped the sleep from our eyes.

Rev and I are proud to have made lots of friends under its roof, including our mate Tony Veg, a guide who invited us to visit his world of veg. He introduced us to heritage tomatoes, grown in a completely organic style with ancient seeds. These are the tomatoes the Tudors used to eat! We've seen the largest watermelons known to man, and tasted at least ten different types of garlic, including French violet garlic, which is bursting with sweet, nutty garlickiness! Probably my favourite curiosity has been the discovery of the Nasturtium root, which has a horseradishy, aniseedy crunch that softens when cooked and gives any one-pot dish some twenty-first century *oomph!* I've included these mighty roots in our Ox Cheek Casserole (see page 121) to highlight their versatility. I *urge* you to seek them out. They can be found, even if you have to browse on the Internet.

Every town will have its own Tony Veg – you just need to search him out. *Enjoy* that search. It's a well-known 'secret' that Morrissey is Manchester's most famous veggie, and we're betting that he is proud of his region's vegetarian roots. Rock on!

CRINKLE-CUT CHIPS

The great British chip is *undoubtedly* a Northern staple. What Northern soul could survive a Saturday night without a wrap of chips for the home journey? It's impossible to contemplate life without them! Believe it or not, most people get chips wrong when cooking them at home. There is only one way to cook them properly and that's doing it *twice*. Up here in the North, we use a 'crinkle-cutter', which does exactly what you'd expect. Crinkle-cut chips have a crispier outer coating, so invest in a cutter if you want the very best.

SERVES 4

4 large potatoes or 5 medium ones

Corn or vegetable oil

Peel your potatoes and use your crinkle-cutter to cut them into 1cm wide sticks. Wash the sticks in plenty of cold water to reduce the starch and pat them dry with a clean tea towel.

Half-fill a clean chip pan, deep-fat fryer or any large pan with oil and heat to 70°C/150°F. Test by carefully dipping in a potato stick to see if it sizzles.

When it's ready, dip the chip basket into the oil, remove and fill with the chips. Lower the basket into the hot oil and fry until they are almost cooked, but not browned (roughly 8 minutes). Remove the basket and turn up the heat to increase the temperature of the oil a little (to 90°C/190°F). Return the basket to the oil and cook until your chips are perfectly brown (another 3–4 minutes). If you don't have a chip basket, remove the chips with a large slotted spoon.

Drain on kitchen roll and serve immediately.

The best potato

There has been a great deal of fervent discussion about the best potato for that perfect chip and the conclusion is, by all reputable accounts, the Maris Piper. Ah, but there are two types of Maris Piper: one type grown in clay and the other in sand. The Lincolnshire Maris Piper is grown in sand, and has the best body, as the sand soaks up the excess water in the spud. Clay-grown Maris Pipers tend to be damper (clay holds water rather than leeching it out of the potato) and less inclined to produce a chip that holds its shape, have a perfectly crunchy exterior and a deliciously light and fluffy interior. Not a lotta people know that!

Serve 'em hot or cold —
with or without vinegar
and in any colour variety.
All we can say is:
More peas, please!

HA-PEA-NESS

PROPER MUSHY PEAS

Mushy peas are as Northern as it comes. Cooked properly, they're a joy to eat and the perfect accompaniment to Fish 'n' Chips. In fact, they're a partnership made in heaven, and don't let anyone tell you otherwise.

The secret of perfect mushy peas is to cook them in a slow cooker. If you prepare them in a pan, the skins tend to separate. Check that your marrowfat peas are well within the best before date or they will be hard. I always do a 250g box of Bigga marrowfats, and soak them overnight with the soaking tablets in the packet. Rinse with a few changes of water the next day. Put them in a slow cooker, cover with 600ml boiling water, and leave for about 4–6 hours or until they're good and soft. They'll be whole, but have a nice bit of thick, sloppy juice. Whatever you do, don't add salt before cooking, or you'll end up with bullets! I like to add a little black pepper and thyme and season with salt *after* the peas are cooked. They're fabulous with a little swirl of mint sauce, too, and they freeze *superbly!* Just warm them gently in the pan after defrosting. If Fish 'n' Chips aren't on the menu, get them out for one of our great plate pies.

PROPER BLACK PEAS

In the autumn, it's a great Northern tradition to cook black peas for Halloween and Bonfire Night parties. We serve 'em in a mug and douse them with malt vinegar, black pepper and a pinch of salt. If you aren't already salivating at the thought, we sure are, just thinking about those generous mugs with the tell-tale juices dripping down the sides. We spoon up heaping mouthfuls, between big bites of hot, creamy potato cooked in the ashes of the bonfire, and finish off with a slab of Parkin. Glorious! Local bonfires were a precious time when Rev and I were kids, and they remain so today. That's one reason why we're *soooo* keen to pass on these simple recipes, to help you recreate your own Northern bonfire experience!

Cook your black peas in exactly the same way as the Mushies. For a party, double the quantities of water and peas, slowly cook throughout the day, and then season to taste for deliciously simple Northern food at its very, very finest!

SAVOY CABBAGE, LEEK & PEA ROAST

This is one of those dishes that should in theory be heavy and stodgy, but is in fact surprisingly light and utterly delicious – something you sneak to the fridge for a second helping of (if there's any left in the first place!)

SERVES 4-6

6–8 large Savoy cabbage leaves

75g unsalted butter

2 tbsp olive oil

6 large leeks, washed, trimmed and finely chopped

3 garlic cloves, peeled and finely chopped

200g Gruyère, grated or Crabtree if you can find it – a wonderful Northern 'Alpine' cheese

180g frozen garden peas (or petits pois if you feel fancy)

½ tsp sugar

Sea salt and freshly ground black pepper

Preheat the oven to 200°C/400°F/Gas mark 6. Take a loaf tin and liberally butter. Set aside.

In a large pan of salted boiling water, blanch the cabbage leaves for 2 minutes. Drain in a colander and pat down with kitchen paper. With a sharp knife, cut out the hard white centres.

Melt 25g of the butter with the olive oil in a large frying pan and add the finely chopped leeks. Keep stirring until they are soft and have a light golden colour. Add the chopped garlic and keep stirring for a few more minutes. Then fold in the cheese till it's thoroughly mixed.

Boil the peas as directed on the packet and once cooked, drain and lightly mash with 25g of the butter, a pinch of salt, the sugar and black pepper. Set aside.

Line a loaf tin with the Savoy cabbage leaves so that they overhang the top. Press half the leek mixture into the tin. Then spoon in the pea mixture and press down. Finish by spooning in the rest of the leek mixture.

Fold over the cabbage leaves to cover the top. Smear the final 25g of butter over the exposed leaves and pop into the oven to cook for 30 minutes or until the top appears golden and glistening.

Gently run a knife around the edge and turn out onto a large plate. Allow to rest for a few minutes before slicing.

TOMATO RISOTTO

After a busy day at the dairy in Garstang, I sometimes carry on up the A6 to the lovely village of Little Eccleston to pick up some beautiful Blackpool tomatoes. This dish perfectly compliments those lovely tomatoes, but we're confident that your own local toms will suffice. This is a great Northern take on a great Northern Italian dish – and we've got lots of Italians up North. Manchester has the second-highest population of Italians in the UK, second only to London, and Italian food became popular there before it reached the rest of the country.

SERVES 4

8 large plum tomatoes

3 whole garlic cloves, peeled

A handful of black olives, pitted

3 sundried tomatoes

2–3 dashes of balsamic vinegar

A pinch of cayenne pepper

A handful of fresh basil leaves

1 tsp salted butter

½ red onion, peeled and finely chopped

2 garlic cloves, peeled and finely chopped

2 celery stalks, finely chopped

1.2 litres homemade chicken stock (see page 62)

300g arborio risotto rice

90ml vermouth

60–90ml single cream

30g Parmesan cheese

Sea salt and freshly ground black pepper

Peel the tomatoes by dropping them into a pan of water that you've brought to the boil and leaving for 8–10 minutes. When you puncture the skin with a sharp knife, it should shrink away and will peel off easily. Halve the tomatoes. Into a liquidiser, place the first seven ingredients. Whizz for 2 minutes and then season to taste with sea salt and black pepper. If it's a little thick, add some water (up to 100ml). That's your sauce done! Next, in a large, deep, frying pan, melt the butter and add your onion, garlic and celery and cook for 2–3 minutes over medium heat until translucent but not coloured.

In a separate pan, simmer your stock. Add your arborio rice to the frying pan and mix into the butter. Add your vermouth and mix again. Using a ladle, add your chicken stock to the rice mixture, one ladleful at a time. Wait until the stock has been absorbed into the rice before adding another.

Stir continuously and, after your third ladle, add some tomato sauce. The quantity you use is completely up to you, but suffice to say that you'll have more than enough in your liquidiser. You can freeze any unused sauce for the next risotto night.

Continue ladling in your chicken stock until the rice is tender, but still has a very slight bite (al dente). Now, season and add your cream. Grate over your Parmesan cheese and then amalgamate all of the ingredients. Want to be sure that it is done to perfection? Put a tablespoon of risotto on a plate and if it settles in a few seconds, it's ready! Plate up and eat instantly, with a crunchy green salad on the side.

SPINACH & POTATO CURRY (SAAG ALOO)

In my opinion, vegetables were *made* for curries. Very rarely will any vegetable taste nicer than in a delicious curry sauce. In fact, I very rarely eat meat curries for that very reason! This Saag Aloo is a combination of lovely green spinach, smooth potatoes and fragrant spices that is both lush and velvety. Best of all, it's easy!

SERVES 6

1.2–1.5 litres water

600g frozen spinach (not fresh)

3 tbsp groundnut oil

1 pinch of ground asafoetida

1 tbsp mustard seeds

110g onions, peeled and halved, then sliced thinly against the grain

5 garlic cloves, peeled and finely chopped

700g floury potatoes, such as King Edwards, peeled and cut into 2cm cubes

1½ tbsp garam masala

3 black cardamom pods

Sea salt

In a saucepan, bring 600ml water to the boil and add the frozen spinach. Cook for 5 minutes to defrost. Drain and leave to one side. Next, in a large, heavy-based curry pan with a lid (or a shallow lidded casserole dish), heat the oil until sizzling. Throw in a pinch of asafoetida and stir for a couple of seconds, then add the mustard seeds and stir until they start to pop. Add the onion and continue cooking, stirring constantly, until it begins to colour. Stir in the garlic and cook for a further 2 minutes.

Add your potato and spinach, and then top with another 600 to 900ml of boiling water. Stir in your garam masala, salt and black cardamoms. Bring to the boil, adding more boiling water if required, and then reduce the heat to a slow simmer. Cover and cook for 60 minutes. The finished result should be almost creamy. Remove the cardamoms.

Serve with two chapattis per person and eat with your fingers. There should be no knives and forks on the table!

THE LIQUIDISER VEGETABLE CURRY

Over the years, I have tasted and watched curries being made by friends and family. I've also seen them made from scratch in the comfort of an Asian home. The truth is that a good 'British' curry can literally take an entire day to prepare. It's a painstaking job, but there is a solution! Below you'll find my curry which takes just *minutes* to prepare, allowing you to relax and enjoy the authentic waft of spices from your kitchen!

SERVES 4

400g tin of tomatoes

1 tbsp ground cumin

1 tbsp ground coriander

1 tsp ground asafoetida

1 tsp ground turmeric

A small bunch of fresh coriander

A large handful of fresh baby spinach

6 garlic cloves, peeled

1–3 fresh green chillies

2.5cm piece of ginger, peeled

3 tbsp groundnut oil

½ cinnamon stick or cassia bark

3 green cardamom pods

2 black cardamom pods

4 cloves

1 tsp fennel seeds

1 tsp black mustard seeds

2 bay leaves

3 potatoes, unpeeled and roughly chopped

3 carrots, unpeeled and roughly chopped

1–2 onions, peeled and chopped

75g frozen garden peas

½ cauliflower, cut into florets

30 green beans, chopped

200ml coconut milk (optional)

Sea salt and black pepper

Into your liquidiser, pour your tin of tomatoes and then fill up the empty tin with water and decant that too. Add the cumin, ground coriander, asafoetida, turmeric, fresh coriander, spinach, garlic, chillies and ginger and put on the lid. Cover the lid with a clean tea towel (this can get messy!) and whizz for 2 minutes.

Next, heat your groundnut oil in your favourite curry pan over medium heat. Add the cinnamon stick, cardamom pods, cloves and fennel seeds and cook for a minute to release the flavours and aroma. After a minute, throw in your mustard seeds and bay leaves and cook until the seeds begin to pop.

Add your vegetables and stir through to introduce them to the spices, then cover with the tomato mixture from the liquidiser. Bring to the boil and then reduce the heat. Simmer for 60 minutes. Season to taste with your salt and pepper. At this point you can use half a tin of coconut milk to thicken and flavour. Warm through and serve with boiled rice or chapattis – or both!

PUDDINGS

O ur puddings up North aren't light and delicate confections with a wisp of spun sugar balanced on top of a smear of jus. On the contrary, they are filling and hearty steam puddings, dumplings and pies made with whatever fruit happens to be in season. How families can stomach a three-course meal of soup, meat course and then a steamed dumpling is beyond me. Personally, I make something like a Jam Roly-Poly for the kids as a mid-afternoon treat and we all just grab a spoon and dive in. We love our puddings and wouldn't be without them.

Puddings are a British invention, I'm glad to say. The original ones were savoury types of sausages such as black pudding (see page 166) and white pudding (made of cereals, suet and breadcrumbs), cooked inside a sausage skin or stomach lining. In the sixteenth century, when houses started to have hot ovens built into the chimneybreast, you could stick a pudding in there while the main course roasted or simmered on the fire below. A pudding cloth replaced the stomach lining for holding ingredients together and during the eighteenth century, sweet ingredients were added to the mix – fruits, jams, sugar – and they began to use lighter sponges as well as the traditional suet batters. Then, in the twentieth century, cooks started to steam puddings in a basin covered with foil and greaseproof paper and immersed in a pan of boiling water. Make the mixture, plonk it in the boiling water and leave it for three hours while you get on with the rest of the meal, just checking occasionally that it hasn't boiled dry. Easy-peasy!

I'm sure if I asked fifty people along the High Street if they know what suet actually is, I wouldn't find one who could tell me. We buy it in innocuous packets nowadays and just add a couple of spoonfuls to our pudding mixture, but the original stuff is in fact the fatty casing around a sheep's kidneys. Yes, you heard that right. I can remember buying a huge chunk of the stuff and grating it to make a steam pudding at my Grandma's. It makes the lushest pudding you've ever tasted – but sadly all that animal fat's not very good for you, so for the recipes in this book I recommend you use vegetarian suet instead.

We Northern kids all grew up having puddings as part of our school dinners, but at our gaff they used to accompany them with pink custard, which would always throw me. It's plain wrong. Custard should be smooth, bright yellow and homemade. You'll find my foolproof recipe on page 35 in the Custard Tart recipe. Don't be tempted to buy custard powder instead because making your own is just as easy. It takes a bit of time because you have to stir it until it thickens, but you'd have to do that with shop bought powder as well and homemade is so much nicer.

Any fruits can be added to my puddings, but I'm particularly big on apples because they keep for longer than soft fruits, providing sustenance through the winter months. We've got loads of tasty varieties up North, such as the Ribston Pippin, which is said to have more vitamin C than any other apple, or the Duke of Devonshire dessert apples, which reach their best after Christmas. Ampleforth Abbey in North Yorkshire grows more than forty varieties of apple. We've got some lovely pears as well, with funky names like the Walton Weeper, Green Slipper and Tongue's Seedling. We grow our own raspberries, strawberries, gooseberries, bilberries and plums, and you can substitute any of these in your pies and crumbles when they're in season. But it's rhubarb that we are best known for. There's more on our world-renowned 'Rhubarb Triangle' on page 209.

One more thing you should know about our Northern pudding habits is that we like a bit of cheese with our fruit – they're the perfect combination. My apple pie has the cheese ready baked in, but if you're offered a chunk of fruit cake up here, you'll likely get a piece of cheese alongside. For a simple and sensational dessert, try grating some Lancashire cheese over piping hot stewed apples or plums, topping with crème fraîche and a sprinkle of brown sugar and toasting under a hot grill – you'll think you've died and gone to heaven.

So there you have it: suet, fruit and cheese are the key ingredients and it's not diet food, but it's good for the soul. When the kids are bickering on a rainy Saturday afternoon, sit them down with a wedge of Northern pudding slathered in creamy custard and peace will descend as if by magic.

BREAD & BUTTER PUDDING

My good friend Lancashire chef Paul Heathcote is famous for his Bread & Butter Pudding and we are delighted to print his fabulous recipe here, but you can taste the real thing at Heathcotes Brasserie in Preston.
A good pudding should have a classic 'wobble' when served, and this one is no exception! In fact, it wobbles with something of a Lancastrian flourish. This is proud Northern food devised by a proud Northern chef.

SERVES 4

For the apricot compote

250ml water

250g dried apricots

1 vanilla pod

Zest of ½ orange

½ cinnamon stick

For the pudding

5 thin slices of white bread

75g unsalted butter

100g sultanas

220ml double cream

220ml full-fat milk

50g caster sugar

1 vanilla pod

3 large free-range eggs

25g icing sugar

50g apricot jam

50g clotted cream, to serve

To make the apricot compote, at least 2 hours before you plan to serve your pudding, bring the water to the boil (a kettle is fine for this). Place your apricots in a heatproof bowl and pour over the boiling water. Leave to stand for about 30 minutes.

Add the remaining ingredients to the apricots, pour into a medium pan and bring to the boil. Reduce the heat and simmer for about 10 minutes, and then leave to cool. Once it is at room temperature, remove the vanilla pod and cinnamon stick, and set to one side.

To make the pudding, preheat the oven to 190°C/375°F/Gas mark 5.

Start making your bread and butter pudding by removing the crusts and then buttering the bread. Place one layer of bread on the base of a 20cm deep tray and cover with a layer of sultanas. Place the rest of the bread on top of the sultanas.

Mix the double cream, milk and sugar together in a pan. Split the vanilla pod and scrape out the seeds into the mixture and bring to the boil. Place the eggs in a separate bowl and whisk the hot liquid into them.

Pour the egg mixture over the bread, place the dish in a bain-marie and put in a moderate oven for about half an hour until cooked.

Dust the pudding with icing sugar and glaze until golden.

Spread the bread and butter pudding thickly with apricot jam and serve with clotted cream and the compote of dried apricots.

We have a saying up North, 'If it ain't broke, don't try and fix it.' Enough said!

SEVEN-CUP STEAMED PUDDING

This genuinely couldn't be simpler to make and it's virtually foolproof. No need for weighing and measuring – just use a standard-sized teacup (250ml). The only thing that can possibly go wrong is letting the pot boil dry while you're steaming, so keep an eye on the water level from time to time. It makes a great Christmas pudding, served with brandy butter and lashings of double cream, or you can dish it up as a rich treat at any time of year with a dollop of custard.

SERVES 4

1 cup breadcrumbs
1 cup self-raising flour
1 cup sugar
1 cup chopped suet
1 cup raisins
1 cup currants
Pinch of mixed spice
1 tbsp treacle
1 egg
1 cup buttermilk
2 tbsp butter

Mix all the dry ingredients with the treacle. Whisk the egg and buttermilk together, add them to the dry ingredients and mix to a stiff dough.

Generously butter the inside of a heatproof bowl and spoon the dough inside. Cover with greaseproof paper, tie a piece of string around the edge just under the rim of the bowl, and lower carefully into a pot of boiling water. Steam for 2½–3 hours, topping up with boiling water if necessary.

Using oven gloves, lift out the bowl. Put a serving plate on top, then upend your pudding onto it. Serve with custard, brandy butter, double cream – or all three.

BAKED APPLE DUMPLINGS

These aren't what you'd normally call 'dumplings' because they're not suet-based. The apples are wrapped in pastry and look dumpling shaped. This is a perfect dish for the kids – to slow them down when they're dashing around like lunatics! But alternatively, the rum gives it a grown-up feel. And it's *lush!*

SERVES 4

450g puff pastry (shop bought is fine)

4 equal-sized apples, peeled and cored (Bramleys or any kind you like)

50g caster sugar, and a little extra to glaze

1 tsp ground cinnamon

100g sultanas

A shot of dark rum for each apple (optional)

1 egg, lightly beaten

Fresh custard, to serve (see the recipe for Custard Tart on page 35 or buy your own)

Preheat the oven to 180°C/350°F/Gas mark 4.

Roll out the pastry on a floured surface and cut into four 25cm circles. Place an apple in the centre of each circle. In a small bowl, mix together the sugar, cinnamon and sultanas and then spoon into the cored centre of each apple. If you're doing the grown-up version, now is the time to pour the rum into the cored centre too.

Moisten the edges of each pastry circle with a little beaten egg, and then gather the pastry up and around each apple, pinching together at the top and pressing down to secure. Turn the dumplings over to hide the pinched pastry beneath. Brush each dumpling with egg and sprinkle with caster sugar.

Place on a greased baking sheet and cook for 30 minutes. The pastry will have risen and it should be a golden brown colour. Serve hot, with lashings of custard.

APPLE CRUMBLE

I have many fond memories of Apple Crumble from my childhood, and can vividly recall my determined tongue working to loosen the gloopy crumble that was stuck to the roof of my mouth. This recipe originated in Wartime Britain, when ingredients were rationed and budgets were tight. Not only is this a good, economical dish, but it's piping hot... and delicious, covered in a thick layer of creamy custard, of course. Only a Northerner can make the word 'crumble' sound so good – 'n that's the end ovvit!

SERVES 4

300g plain flour

Pinch of salt

175g Demerara sugar

2 tbsp caster sugar

200g unsalted butter, at room temperature, plus a little extra to grease and dot on top

450g apples, peeled, cored and chopped into chunks (Bramleys or any kind you like)

50g soft brown sugar

Pinch and a bit of ground cinnamon

Homemade custard, to serve

Preheat the oven to 180°C/350°F/Gas mark 4.

In a large mixing bowl, blend together the flour, salt, Demerara sugar and caster sugar. Cut your butter into cubes and, using your fingertips, massage into the flour mixture, a few cubes at a time. Carry on until you have a mixture that looks like breadcrumbs. Set to one side.

Place your apple in a large saucepan with a few drops of water to help them 'fall', and turn your heat to medium. When the apples begin to break down, with a little help from a wooden spoon, turn the heat to low. Stir in the brown sugar and cinnamon and let the apple chunks stew until they look like glorious, gooey pieces.

Turn your apples into a greased ovenproof dish with a diameter of roughly 20cm, sprinkle over the crumble mixture, and dot with a little butter. Bake for 40–45 minutes, until the crumble is nicely browned and the apples are bubbling.

Serve piping hot with a good dollop of homemade custard on top. Enjoy the hush around the table as everybody tucks in.

LANCASHIRE CHEESE & APPLE PIE

It's long been recognised that a slice of cheese goes beautifully with a great apple pie, but did you know that adding Lancashire cheese to the pastry makes it simply amazing? This recipe *really* works and makes the most fitting end to a fabulous Northern Sunday lunch on any special occasion. Be warned: without custard, this dish is like Fred Astaire without Ginger Rogers!

SERVES 6

50g unsalted butter

4 large Bramley apples, peeled and roughly chopped (not too small) – or you can use any firm apple you like

2 tbsp soft brown sugar

A pinch or two of freshly ground black pepper

1 tsp cinnamon

250g Lancashire cheese, thinly sliced

1 tsp fresh sage, finely chopped

1 free-range egg, lightly beaten

Fresh custard and single cream, to serve

For the pastry

250g plain flour

A pinch of salt

50g butter, chilled

25g lard or butter

30g Lancashire crumbly cheese, crumbled

Preheat the oven to 190°C/375°F/Gas mark 5.

To make the pastry, sift the flour and salt into a mixing bowl. Cut the butter and lard into cubes and add to the flour, then rub between your fingertips until you achieve a fine breadcrumb consistency. Add the cheese. Gradually mix in a little cold water until all traces of flour are removed from the side of the bowl and your pastry is moist (not sticky or crumbly). Add a little more flour if it becomes too sticky and a little more water if it crumbles. Roll your pastry into a ball, chuck it in a plastic bag and refrigerate for 30 minutes.

In a large saucepan, melt your butter and then stir in the chopped apple, sugar, black pepper and cinnamon. Cover and cook over a medium heat for 8–10 minutes until they have reduced down, but you can still see the shape of the apple pieces. Tip into a bowl to cool.

Separate the pastry into two portions – one of two-thirds and the other one-third – and roll out. Line a loose-bottomed 24cm baking tin with the larger sheet of pastry and trim the edges. Top with cheese, then cover with the cooled apple mixture. Moisten the top edge of the pastry with a little water, and cover with your second sheet of pastry before trimming to fit. Crimp the edges with a fork and then brush the top of your pie with beaten egg.

Place in the oven and bake for 35–40 minutes, or until the pastry is a nice golden brown. Allow to cool slightly and turn it out before cutting. Serve with a little cream and some fresh custard.

JAM ROLY-POLY

Back in the nineteenth century, these were known as 'Dead Man's Arm' or 'Dead Man's Leg' (for obvious, if somewhat gory, reasons); either that or Shirt Sleeve Pudding because they'd steam it wrapped in an old shirt. No Northern cookbook could be complete without the lush Jam Roly-Poly. It would be plain stupid to ignore this joyous mix of suet and raspberry jam, smothered in homemade custard, of course. It's the archetypal school dinner food!

SERVES 4–6

250g self-raising flour

A pinch of salt

125g shredded suet

4 tbsp raspberry jam, warmed

A little milk, for brushing

1 free-range egg, beaten, for brushing

Caster sugar, to glaze

Homemade custard, to serve

Preheat the oven to 200°C/400°F/Gas mark 6.

Sift the flour and salt into your favourite mixing bowl. Stir in the suet and enough water (6–8 tbsp) to make a soft, but not too sticky, dough. Turn out on a floured surface and roll out a rectangle, about 30 x 20cm. Brush the pastry with warm jam, leaving a 1cm border around the edge of the rectangle. Fold the pastry border inwards and brush with milk or egg.

With the short side of your rectangle before you, gently roll the pastry away from you, creating a magnificent Swiss roll. Carefully seal the ends and place on a greased baking tray with the sealed edge underneath. Brush with beaten egg and sprinkle with caster sugar.

Bake for about 35–40 minutes until golden brown. Remove from the oven and sprinkle with a little more sugar. Serve piping hot with homemade custard. Heaven onna plate!

STICKY TOFFEE PUDDING

If there's one thing my kids are experts on, it's Sticky Toffee Pudding, and when we did a recent blind taste test, this is the one they chose. Hands down, no question, the winner. Some versions have treacle in them, but I think this makes it too rich. Always serve with a scoop of vanilla ice cream for the hot-and-cold effect, and be careful not to burn your mouth on the caramel. One final tip: When we had a sticky toffee pudding competition, the winner used cinder toffee, which got the 'stickiness' that's needed.

200g stoned dates, finely chopped

1 tsp baking powder

300ml boiling water

50g unsalted butter, softened to room temperature

80g golden caster sugar

80g dark muscovado sugar

2 eggs, beaten

1 tsp vanilla essence (if you don't have a vanilla pod in your sugar bowl)

175g plain flour

40g cinder toffee (like honeycomb; it's optional, so don't worry if you can't find it)

Sauce

115g unsalted butter

75g golden caster sugar

40g dark muscovado sugar

140ml double cream

Make the sauce first. Melt all the sauce ingredients together in a pan, bring to the boil and boil evenly for 4 minutes. Pour half the sauce into an ovenproof dish that is about 20cm square and 5cm deep. Put it in the freezer.

Place the stoned dates and baking powder in the boiling water in a measuring jug and leave for 15–20 minutes while you prepare the rest of the pudding.

Preheat the oven to 180°C/350°F/Gas mark 4.

Mix the butter, caster sugar and muscovado sugar together in a bowl using a wooden spoon until they are light and fluffy. This takes a fair bit of elbow grease! Stir in the eggs, the vanilla essence (if using) and then sift in the flour. Whisk until the batter is even, then liquidise for 30 seconds in a liquidiser. Lightly crush the cinder toffee, if using, and add to the batter.

Pour your batter over the ovenproof dish that has been in the freezer and put it in the oven for 30 minutes.

Take out your pudding and poke it ten or twelve times with a skewer, creating holes all the way to the bottom. Pour over the remainder of the sauce so it seeps down into the holes, then serve with a scoop of vanilla ice cream.

ORANGE GINGER TRIFLE

This trifle is wonderfully rich and caramelly and has a fiery kick from the ginger biscuits. I've used Grasmere Gingerbread biscuits, which have been produced in the famous Ambleside village of Grasmere since the 1860s. The sugar shards look dramatic and cut through the cream and custard, making it even more delicious the next day. I promise this will be the best trifle you've ever tasted. There's nothing trifling about this trifle.

4 Grasmere Gingerbread biscuits (or any good-quality ginger biscuit)

6 trifle sponges

6 oranges

4 tbsp Cointreau

300ml custard. A good-quality supermarket custard will do and makes life simple.

200ml double cream

200ml single cream

145g caster sugar

Place the gingerbread biscuits in a plastic bag and smash to crumbs with a rolling pin.

Place the trifle sponges in a glass trifle bowl. Sprinkle with the gingerbread crumbs.

Squeeze the juice of three of the oranges over the sponges and crumbs. Pour over the Cointreau. Peel off thin strips of orange peel from one of the squeezed oranges and add to the sponge/crumbs/Cointreau.

With a sharp knife, finely slice the three remaining oranges and place the slices over the sponge. Cover with the custard.

Pour the double and single cream into a bowl and whisk until it's thick and peaky. Use a spatula to spread over the custard. Place the trifle in the fridge for at least 3 hours.

Now, the magic. Put the caster sugar in a pan over a high heat. Melt until the sugar turns mid-brown and is caramelised. Don't over-cook or it will burn and taste horrible.

Line a shallow tray with silver foil and pour the melted sugar onto it. It should be about 2mm thick. Allow to cool and then gently take a rolling pin to it, breaking the pane of sugar into 'shards'.

Just before you're ready to serve, stick the shards of sugar into the cream top of the trifle.

PEAR, BLUE CHEESE & ROSEMARY TARTS

There is something special about the flavour of sweet, ripe pears combined with a good blue cheese, and this is a pudding and cheese course all rolled into one! We love our cheese and fruit together up North, and these divine, sweetly savoury tarts are no exception – a match made in heaven. Serve at the end of a meal – or even as a scrumptious starter, on a bed of rocket.

SERVES 4

250g Smelly Ha'peth or your own favourite blue cheese

2 small free-range eggs, whites only

1 tbsp crème fraîche

500g shortcrust pastry (shop bought or see Cheese 'n' Onion Pie page 90)

1 tbsp fresh rosemary leaves, finely chopped, plus a little more to garnish

50g salted butter

2 large, ripe (but firm) pears, peeled, cored and cut into 1cm slices

1 tbsp caster sugar

1 tsp cumin seeds

Sea salt and freshly ground black pepper, to taste

In a mixing bowl, mash the cheese lightly with a fork. Whisk the egg whites until just frothy and add to the cheese with the crème fraîche. Mix until you have a coarse paste. Season with salt and pepper and then refrigerate for 10 minutes.

Grease four 12.5cm loose-bottomed tart tins (the ones with the fluted edges are best).

On a floured surface, roll out your pastry to about 3mm thick and line the tart tins. Trim the edges and prick well with a fork. Carefully spread the cheese mixture into the tart tins and sprinkle with the chopped rosemary. Return to the fridge.

Next, melt your butter in a heavy-bottomed pan and then add your pear slices, sugar and enough water to create a light syrup around the pears (about 60ml). Cook gently for about 6–8 minutes, uncovered, until the pears are tender and you have an unctuous syrupy sauce. Remove from the heat and leave to cool.

Preheat the oven to 200°C/400°F/Gas mark 6.

Remove the tarts from the tins and arrange the pear slices on top in a neat overlapping circle. Brush with a little melted butter, sprinkle over the cumin seeds and a scattering of rosemary, season with sea salt and pepper and then cook for 15–20 minutes until golden. Allow the tarts to cool slightly before scoffing down!

BROWN BREAD ICE CREAM

One of the best ice cream recipes ever! It's important to keep an eye on the bread and the sugar when they're under the grill to make sure they reach *just* the right level of caramelisation – take your eye off it and it's back to the drawing board! Having said that, this recipe is great fun and you'll soon realise that any trickiness is worthwhile! The end result is a decadently creamy taste of a good Northern childhood. *Delightful!*

SERVES 4

240ml double cream

30g vanilla caster sugar (leave a vanilla pod in a jar of caster sugar for a couple of days)

85g brown breadcrumbs

85g soft brown sugar

Preheat your grill to a high heat.

In a small bowl, whip the cream and caster sugar together until well blended. Turn out onto a tray and place in the freezer.

After about 20-30 minutes, the mixture should have started to harden. Using a palette knife, fold the mixture into the middle and flatten out again. Place back in the freezer.

Meanwhile, lay the breadcrumbs out on a baking tray and sprinkle with brown sugar.

Place the breadcrumbs under the hot grill and watch like a hawk. You want them caramelised, and all the sugar melted, but not burnt. Stir from time to time to make sure everything is getting evenly cooked.

Once done, take the breadcrumbs out from under the grill and set aside. Leave to cool, then break the caramelised mixture up using your fingers or a rolling pin.

Take the ice cream out of the freezer and mix in the caramelised breadcrumbs.

Spoon the mixture into a suitable dish or individual ramekins and place back in the freezer. Wait till frozen.

Brown bread with nowt tekken out! Glorious for a special dinner party, a family meal or even a garden treat on a hot summer's day.

PICKLES, JAMS, DRINKS & ACCOMPANIMENTS

Northerners see nothing wrong with having a bit on the side – in fact, we think it's essential! Every good meal is served on a table groaning with jars and bottles of condiments that don't so much mask the flavour of our food, but give it depth and bite! We live for relishes, hot and sweet sauces, fruity jams and jellies, spicy warming mustards and feisty pickles, and no menu is complete without bottles of brown sauce, tomato ketchup, good-quality malt vinegar, curry sauce and, a Northern favourite, Henderson's Relish, lined up to do the business.

Our pickles are divine, and make use of some of our finest produce, including carrots, tomatoes, beetroot, apples, pears, plums, red onions, peaches and sweet corn. We zest them up with Asian ingredients such as ginger, limes and super-hot chillies, and stir in some fine Northern ales, rum and whisky to round them off. Mouths of steel, we have, and the hotter the better! You'll not go far in the North before encountering a jar of Piccalilli, another Northern favourite that borrows a few tricks from India, but try my recipe on page 204, which is streets ahead of any shop bought one.

We slather our bread 'n' butter with jams, curds and jellies. My own jam recipe uses Vimto, our favourite cordial, to give it a kick. And don't miss out on my Rhubarb Curd (see page 210), made with our very own Yorkshire forced rhubarb. It's the business.

Be sure to leave room on the table for a glass as well. We like our booze in the North, but we're not secretive drinkers – it's always been a sociable thing. Back in the nineteenth century, the tradition of working mens' clubs started up here, when men came out of the gates of the newly built factories and wanted somewhere to get together for a cheap pint and a natter. The clubs were private, non-profit organisations run by their members, where there was a bar, snooker and pool tables, and weekend entertainments, usually music or comedy. They would hand out charity as well if anyone fell on especially hard times. Only men were allowed in the bar and the games room but there might be a separate lounge for the poor chaps who'd been coerced into bringing the wife along. This began to change in the mid-twentieth century as Women's Libbers challenged it, but until the mid 1970s, Rev's mum was only allowed into her husband's club on Saturday nights.

The 'turns' at some clubs were world famous. The renowned Batley Variety Club hosted Louis Armstrong, Engelbert Humperdinck, the Bee Gees, Roy Orbison and Dusty Springfield. At Manchester's Embassy Club, the resident comedian was the non-PC Bernard Manning, who played to packed crowds of all nationalities despite his somewhat dodgy jokes. Young comedians stood up in working men's clubs to try out their material, but needed to be thick-skinned to deal with the abuse (and drinks) that could be hurled at them if they bombed. As they grew, you started getting tickets for dinner as well as the cabaret, and in the 60s and 70s if you were lucky it would be 'chicken in a basket' – tasty fried chicken legs served with piles of chips that everyone tucked into, wiping greasy fingers on piles of paper napkins. The drink was beer, of course; none of those fancy G & Ts like you got in the posh clubs down South. And at the end of the night everyone stood on the tables for the last act. I love that! Bet there were a few tumbles...

Working men's clubs have been closing down over the last few decades as people make their own entertainment at home, with TV, DVDs and barbecues. The megastars now play arena concerts to tens of thousands instead of a few hundred in an intimate club atmosphere, which is a crying shame, if you ask me. There's a thriving new club scene in our big cities, though, mostly based around the music, and you'll find plenty of swanky cocktail bars in Manchester, Sheffield, Newcastle and Leeds. However, you don't get communities and generations mixing there the way they did at the old social clubs. It's all change...

I've been researching the subject of ales for almost three decades and I can tell you that (in my not-so-humble opinion) our ales are still the best in the world. Northerners had a go at growing vines, but the elements were against us (don't let that stop you from serving a decent Bordeaux with your roast dinner and Yorkies or a cheeky Sancerre with your scallops). In this section, you'll find some seriously moreish cocktails to impress your mates, using a range of good old Northern ingredients from Newkie Brown to strawberries in season. And don't miss Rev's ingenious recipes for drinking your favourite sweets. We boldly go where no other cookbook would dare!

Whatever your tipple, if you want to make it Northern, just make it sociable. Call the neighbours in to watch the footie and crack open a few cans; get the girls round for a good old gas over a jug of Strawberry Fizzler; or throw a party where you just pour whatever anyone brings into the potluck punch, occasionally diluting it with a splash of Vimto. Cheers!

PICCALILLI

If you ask me, a classic Northern sandwich goes something like this: Oven-Bottom Muffins (see page 38) filled with Lancashire crumbly cheese and Piccalilli! In my opinion, this is an all-time winner, and the Piccalilli is just as important as the cheese and the bread. It's also a perfect partner for the Raised Pork Pie (see page 86), Pig in a Ginnel (see page 156) and Midsummer Ham Hock Terrine (see page 159).

MAKES 3-4 PINT JARS

2 whole cauliflowers, cut into very small florets

8 large onions, peeled and diced

Plenty of sea salt (about 75g)

2 cucumbers, peeled, deseeded and diced

600ml white wine vinegar

300ml malt vinegar

8 fresh chillies (your choice)

50g ground turmeric

50g mustard powder

350g caster sugar

3 tbsp cornflour

1 tbsp fresh coriander, very finely chopped (optional)

Place your cauliflower and onion in a large bowl, cover with 50g of the salt and leave for 24 hours.

When you are ready to make your Piccalilli, place your cucumber in a bowl, add 25g salt and leave for 30 minutes. Pour both vinegars into a saucepan with the chillies and boil. Take off the heat and leave to ferment for 30 minutes.

In a small bowl, blend together all of the dry ingredients. When your chilli-vinegar mixture has cooled, pour a little into the bowl and stir. Bring the remainder of the vinegar mixture back to the boil and stir in your dry ingredients until you have a full, smooth, yellow sauce.

Rinse your cauliflower, onion and cucumber thoroughly and stir into the sauce. Add extra water to make a nice creamy consistency like a good custard and stir in up to 3 further tablespoons of mustard powder to thicken, if required. Add the very finely chopped coriander. Decant into sterilised jars, either with a rubber seal or a screwtop, and store. The Piccalilli will keep for 1 or 2 weeks after opening, and at least 7–8 weeks unopened. A little bit of somethin' on the side!

THE PERFECT GRAVY

In all my years of collecting cookbooks, I've never found a recipe for perfect gravy in any of them – and us Northerners just love our gravy. This is the traditional Great Northern way of making gravy, the one all mothers teach their children. It's rich, brown and meaty, just what you need on your pie while you're watching *Soccer AM* on the telly.

SERVES THE WHOLE
FAMILY

Juices from your roast

1 tbsp plain flour

A splash of good balsamic
vinegar

2–3 dashes of Worcestershire
sauce

Sea salt and freshly ground
black pepper

While your meat is resting, scrape the scrummy, caramelised goodness from the bottom of the roasting tin with a wooden spoon. Mix in the flour and place your roasting tin across two rings of your hob. Very slowly add hot water (the water from boiling your veggies is ideal), a couple of tablespoons at a time, and gently stir in. Continue to add water and whisk to get rid of any lumps. Add your balsamic vinegar and the Worcestershire sauce to colour your gravy and bring out the flavour. At this point, your gravy should be nice and thick!

Slowly add about 300ml hot water and bring the whole lot to the boil. Reduce the temperature to a gentle simmer for about 20 minutes to reduce the gravy and intensify the flavour. Season to taste and then sieve before serving in a warm gravy boat. It's perfect, all right!

TOMATO KETCHUP

Kids and adults alike love tomato ketchup and there is nothing finer or more satisfying than homemade. This recipe originally comes from *The Big Red Book of Tomatoes* by Lindsey Bareham, more recently via Hugh Fearnley-Whittingstall's *The River Cottage Cookbook*. This is one recipe that gets around – and for obvious reasons. When you see tomatoes on offer, it's time to make enough of this gorgeous ketchup to see you through the month. There you go: cheap as chips and the best way to accompany them!

MAKES LOTS OF BOTTLES

3kg ripe plum tomatoes, roughly chopped

3 onions, peeled and sliced

1 large red pepper, seeds and white membrane removed, chopped

100g soft brown sugar

200ml cider vinegar

¼ tsp mustard powder

1 cinnamon stick

1 tsp allspice

1 tsp whole cloves

1 tsp ground mace

1 tsp celery seeds

1 tsp black peppercorns

2 bay leaves

1 garlic clove, peeled and bruised

Sea salt

Paprika

In a large pan, add the tomato, onion and red pepper and cook over medium heat, stirring occasionally, for approximately 15 minutes until very soft. Push through a coarse-mesh sieve and return to the pan with the sugar, vinegar and mustard.

Tie the cinnamon, allspice, cloves, mace, celery seeds, black peppercorns, bay leaves and garlic in a square of muslin and chuck into the pan. Bring to the boil and then reduce to a slow simmer. Cook, allowing it to bubble gently and stirring often, for 20–40 minutes.

Make sure you taste a couple of times throughout the cooking process, removing the spice bag if the flavour becomes too strong. When it's thick and pulpy, it's ready. Season to taste with salt and paprika, then leave to cool.

Take a large funnel and pour the ketchup into sterilised, suitable bottles and seal. Once opened, keep in the fridge for up to a month.

In the (almost) words of Johnny Kidd & the Pirates: 'Shake it all over!'

VIMTO JAM

Vimto cordial was invented just over 100 years ago by John Noel Nichols of Blackburn, is now produced on Merseyside and is peculiar to the North. This curious fruit squash, laced with herbs and spices, can be enjoyed hot or cold and it is delicious frozen as ice lollies. I decided to try something slightly different, creating a recipe for a good Northern jam that makes great use of lovely British berries. For those of you who have never tried Vimto before, please, please, please go and buy a bottle! You'll need a breadmaker with a jam setting for this recipe. If you try to do it on the hob, you'll be stuck there stirring it the whole time.

MAKES 2 PINT JARS

A punnet each of strawberries, blackberries, blueberries and raspberries

Pectin sugar (half the weight of the fruit)

100ml Vimto cordial

Place all of the ingredients into the pan of your breadmaker, insert into the machine and programme accordingly. After 85 minutes, you will have the most gorgeous jam. Allow to cool slightly and then spoon into sterilised jars and refrigerate. It will last for up to 2 months unopened, and 2-3 weeks after opening. *Jamtastic!*

Amazingly versatile and melt-in-your-mouth delicious, our Northern rhubarb is the business.

THE RHUBARB TRIANGLE

Most of the UK's rhubarb is grown in the triangular area between Leeds, Bradford and Wakefield, where acres and acres of forcing sheds have been built to accommodate it. The industry started about 150 years ago when miners in pit villages started putting a few stalks of 'tusky' alongside the potatoes in their allotments. They had to be covered with buckets to keep them pink and tender, but they seemed to do well in Yorkshire soil, and so the business grew. By the 1920s there were over two hundred rhubarb growers creeping around their forcing sheds by candlelight (strong lights make the stalks lose their deep pink colour) and exporting their produce far and wide. Cheaper imports hurt trade in the 1960s and several growers went out of business, but there are still a dozen major Yorkshire growers producing 1,000 tons of the pink stuff every year.

The leaves of the rhubarb plant are poisonous, and only the stems are eaten. Tender early crops from January to April don't need to be trimmed before use, but the main crop, from March to June, is tougher and more acidic. Chop it into bits and poach or stew with sugar to taste – plus a bit of ginger or orange if you want to be fancy. When we were kids, we'd eat raw stalks of rhubarb dipped into a poke of sugar and we'd be happy as sandboys.

We like our festivals and competitions up North, so there's an annual Rhubarb Festival in Wakefield with cookery demonstrations and plenty of goodies to sample and buy. We're all familiar with rhubarb crumbles and pies, but have you ever tried rhubarb jam, rhubarb chutney or rhubarb fool? Try our Rhubarb Curd recipe on page 210 for a taste of what you could be missing.

There's rhubarb grown in other parts of Britain, and other parts of the world, but the Yorkshire forced crop is uniquely tasty. That's why it now has a Protected Designation of Origin status, which means that only rhubarb grown within the Rhubarb Triangle can be given the name Yorkshire rhubarb. It's well worth a visit to the area, where they offer tours of some of their forcing sheds. If you listen carefully you'll actually be able to hear the rhubarb growing, as a little membrane around the leaves pops as it unfurls. Spooky stuff!

RHUBARB CURD

Rhubarb has a special place in the hearts of Northerners and can still be found in gardens and allotments all over the North. Forced Yorkshire Rhubarb, which should be Barbie pink, is our local speciality. As Janet Oldroyd, one the few remaining growers, says, 'The soil's to be right, the climate's to be right and everything comes together here in Yorkshire.'

MAKES 4-6 JARS

450g rhubarb, washed, trimmed and cut into 2cm chunks

450g granulated sugar

125g butter, cut into chunks

Juice and zest of 1 lemon

4 free-range egg yolks

Heat the rhubarb in a pan with 100g of the sugar and 4 tbsp water for 10 minutes. Once the rhubarb turns soft, purée with a liquidiser.

Put the butter, remaining sugar, lemon juice and zest and rhubarb mixture into a double boiler or a heatproof bowl over a pan of simmering water. Stir. As soon as the sugar has dissolved and the mixture has turned hot and glossy, but before it is too hot – you don't want it to boil – add the eggs by putting them through a sieve and whisking them into the hot mixture with a balloon sieve.

If the rhubarb mixture is too hot, the egg will split. If this happens, take it off the heat and whisk vigorously until smooth again.

Keep stirring over a gentle heat for another 10 minutes until the mixture has turned thick and creamy.

Pour into 4–6 sterilised jars (old jam jars will do), seal with sterilised screwtops and leave to cool. Use within 4 weeks and, once opened, keep the jar in the fridge and use within 2 weeks (I promise it will be gone before that).

Sterilising jars

Old jam jars and their lids can be sterilised easily. Just wash the jars in kitchen detergent and rinse. Then place them in a warmed oven – 170°C/325°F/Gas mark 3 will do it – for a few minutes. Let them cool down before you take them out. The lids can be washed and rinsed by hand.

DRINKS

NO COAT 'N' KNICKERS 'CHAMPAGNE' COCKTAIL

It might be minus five outside, but come Saturday night, there isn't a coat in sight north of Birmingham. For Saturday night girls who wanna have fun, this is the perfect drink. It's easy on the purse, whilst looking 'dead sophisticated'. Ostensibly a 'poor man's champagne cocktail', to my mind, it's as good as the real thing.

PER GLASS

1 sugar cube
Splash of Angostura Bitters
A measure (25ml) apple schnapps or apple liqueur
Strong white cider, to top up

In a champagne glass, place a sugar cube. Splash with Angostura bitters.

Pour in a measure of apple schnapps or apple liqueur and top up with strong white cider.

NEWKIE BROWN PUNCH

My drama student days were all about Newcastle Brown Ale, gigs at the Hacienda in Manchester and long hours spent in the library, of course. This punch will really get the party started, whether you're a student or not. The recipe might sound like the contents of the back of the larder, but it really does the trick.

SERVES 3–4

1 tin of condensed milk
2 tins of 'nourishment' protein drink
2 bottles of Newcastle Brown Ale
A glug of rum
A pinch of powdered cinnamon
A good pinch of mixed spice
A little grated nutmeg, to decorate

Put all the ingredients in a large mixing bowl and stir thoroughly – taste as you stir and if you need more 'spice', just keep adding. Serve over ice in long glasses with some grated nutmeg to decorate or, if you're feeling really posh, it works in cocktail glasses too.

POTTER'S PUNCH

Alnwick Castle has of course played host to the Harry Potter movies, so I wanted to create a classic punch that celebrates that. I'm sure Harry is old enough now to enjoy this tipple – in moderation, of course.

SERVES 1

60ml dark rum
15ml Martini Rosso
A splash of Angostura Bitters
Equal parts of fresh orange juice and fresh pineapple juice (about 60ml each)
Fresh mint, to serve

Pour the dark rum, Martini Rosso and Bitters over ice in a tall glass. Stir well. Top up with equal parts of fresh orange juice and pineapple juice. Add fresh mint to garnish if you fancy. Go on – put an umbrella and sparkler in it too! This is a seriously fun drink.

A NEWCASTLE NIGHTCAP

Rev and I spend much of our time travelling from food show to food show around the north of England. It's early starts and early to bed for the most part. This nightcap is a favourite, though it sometimes has the opposite effect and gets the party started all over again. So be warned!

SERVES 1

60ml cream sherry

2 tbsp single cream

1 tsp dark muscovado sugar

1 egg

Nutmeg, to serve

Put all the ingredients, except the nutmeg, in a cocktail shaker with ice and give it a good shake. Pour into martini glasses and serve with a sprinkling of nutmeg. Creamy and delicious.

STRAWBERRY FIZZLER

Once you've stuffed your face with strawberries out in the field, devoured them with cream and sugar back at home and made enough jam to last the recession – try this. I think it would be great for a wedding or special occasion party.

SERVES 8–10

2 punnets of strawberries

80g caster sugar

1 lemon

1 bottle of cheap white wine

A splash of brandy

1 bottle of cheap fizz

Fresh mint, to garnish

Halve the strawberries, put in a bowl and sprinkle with sugar. Peel off thin strips of lemon peel and squeeze the lemon. Add to the strawberries and place in the fridge for a couple of hours or overnight.

Pour the white wine and splash of brandy over the strawberries and refrigerate for a further hour.

Shortly before serving, add the cheap fizz and serve in champagne glasses. Decorate with mint leaves.

REV'S VODKA SHOTS

Rev used to work flavouring vodkas for a popular firm and once he realised how simple it was, he began creating his own. Here are two versions of his amazing vodka shots: one using boiled sweets and another using chocolate. Both can be stored in the freezer.

135–150g boiled sweets
    OR 135–150g milk or dark chocolate
750ml bottle of vodka

For the boiled-sweet shots, place your sweets in your food processor and zap until you have a fine powder.

Pour your vodka into a deep pudding bowl and tip in the powdered sweets. Microwave on full power for 1 minute. Remove and mix thoroughly until the sweets have melted into the vodka. Return to the microwave for another minute on full power.

Remove the bowl and sieve the vodka back into the vodka bottle, using a muslin cloth or a fine sieve and a funnel. Freeze the whole bottle overnight and serve beautifully chilled!

For the chocolate shots, break up your chocolate and place in a deep pudding bowl. Tip in the bottle of vodka and microwave on full power for 1 minute. Remove and mix thoroughly until the chocolate has melted into the vodka. Return to the microwave for another minute on full power.

Place the pudding bowl in the freezer and leave overnight. By morning, all of the fat from the chocolate will have risen to the surface. Skim it off and then sieve the chocolatey vodka into the bottle, as above. until ready to serve.

THE BULLSHOT

Back in the nineteenth century, the Northern gentry used to sip this savoury alcoholic drink from their hip flasks whilst out hunting. Sometimes it's served warm or, as a cocktail, over ice. And whilst it's definitely an acquired taste, this version goes perfectly with The Northern Gentleman's Afternoon Tea (see page 44). A couple of dashes of Henderson's Relish is traditional and a speciality of Yorkshire. It's sold at The Yorkshire Pantry in York (www.theyorkshirepantry.com) and you can also use the more familiar Midlands' version, Worcestershire sauce.

SERVES 2

45ml vodka
75ml beef consommé (tinned beef consommé is traditional)
Juice of 1 lemon wedge
2 dashes of Henderson's Relish
2 dashes of Tabasco sauce

Mix all the ingredients together. Serve in short glasses over ice or alternatively, share among shot glasses for a quick invigorating hit before you tuck into The Northern Gentleman's Tea (page 44).

The Real Ale Revolution
is putting those imported
imposters right where they
belong – and that's not
round here!

FAVOURITE ALES

According to legend, in the Middle Ages an 'Ale Conner' was a kind of early tax collector, whose job it was to test the quality and strength of the beer – not by drinking it, but by sitting in it! They travelled from pub to pub, wearing leather britches. Beer was poured on a wooden bench and the Ale Conner sat in it. Depending upon how sticky it was when they stood up, they could assess its alcoholic strength and impose a relevant tax.

Rev and I are equally enthusiastic travellers, and being big fans of Real Ale, we like nothing better than to test the stuff ourselves – by pouring it down our throats rather than on our barstools! The Real Ale revolution has swept the nation, and it's putting imported beers firmly in their place. There are some absolutely gorgeous beers up here in the North, where the purity of the water and the quality of the grains are second to none. While researching this book, Rev and I were amazed by the diversity of the beer-making process and tastes. We've already adopted a few favourites. Take, for example, Timothy Taylor's 'Landlord' bitter, brewed in Keighley, Yorkshire. It's simply sublime, creamy Real Ale at its finest. Travel a few miles up the road to North Yorkshire, and you can sample the Black Sheep Brewery's delicious ale. A little further on, towards Tadcaster, you'll find the new home of Newcastle Brown Ale. The company moved here in 2009, after 83 years of brewing their

award-winning brown ale on Tyneside. It's nutty brown and lush as 'oot!

Cross the country to the west, and you'll find yourself in Cumbria, where some of their many beers include those from the Hawkshead Brewery (a craft brewery producing traditional Cumbrian ales with a modern twist, in the heart of the Lake District) and the Jennings Brewery, which was founded in the village of Lorton (between Keswick and Cockermouth) in 1828 by John Jennings. Both produce some divine libations, too good to miss!

Heading southwards to our home city of Manchester, you'll find a host of micro breweries en route, which include a couple of our favourites: The Millstone Brewery, The Greenfield Brewery and the Marble Arch Brewery. Take our word for it: Real Ale is the new Rock 'n' Roll, and if you don't believe us, just ask Madonna what *her* favourite ale is (rumour suggests that it's Timothy Taylor's Landlord bitter).

Lots of gastropubs in the North now suggest the beer you should drink with each dish and if you're from out of town, it's well worth listening to their advice. Some even offer to serve you in 'thirds': a third of a pint with each course.

USEFUL RESOURCES

Northern food markets

Ashton-under-Lyne
every day but Sunday

Bury
Wednesdays/Fridays/Saturdays

Bolton
Tuesdays/Thursdays/Fridays/
Saturdays

Skipton
Mondays/Wednesdays/Fridays/
Saturdays

**New Smithfield Market –
Manchester**
Saturday 2:30am–11:30am

**Arndale Fish Market –
Manchester**
every day

Northern restaurant reviews

www.squidbeak.co.uk

Cheesemakers

Saddleworth (that's us!)
www.saddleworthcheese.co.uk

Wensleydale
www.wensleydale.co.uk

Swaledale
www.swaledalecheese.co.uk

Leagram Dairy
www.ribblevalleyfoodtrail.com/
leagram-organic-dairy.htm

Carron Lodge
www.carronlodge.com

**Pextenement Organic
Cheese, Todmorden,
West Yorkshire**
www.pextenement.co.uk

**Dewlay Cheesemakers,
Garstang**
www.dewlay.com

**Lacey's Cheese Ltd,
Richmond, North Yorkshire
(tiny, artisan maker)**
www.laceyscheese.co.uk

**The Ribblesdale Cheese
Company, Hawes**
www.yorkshiredalescheeses.co.uk

**Larkton Hall Farm
(for Alpine cheese)**
For stockists, email peter.
clayton@claytonpartnership.co.uk

Fish

C & G Neve, Fleetwood
www.directseafoods.co.uk/index.
php/our-depots/neve-fleetwood

**Fortune Smokehouse
in Whitby**
www.fortuneskippers.co.uk

**L Robson's Craster Kippers,
Northumberland**
www.kipper.co.uk

**Mackenzies Smokehouse
in Nidderdale smokes pretty
much everything
(fish, poultry, game)**
www.yorkshiresmokehouse.co.uk

**Bleikers have been around
for decades**
www.bleikerssmokehouse.co.uk

**Port of Lancaster
Smokehouse**
www.lancastersmokehouse.co.uk

Pies

**Pork Pie Appreciation
Society**
www.theoldbridgeinn.co.uk

Denby Dale pies
www.denbydalepie.com

Northern meats

East Wingates Farm,
Northumberland (for lamb)
www.thelambman.com

Alf Pearson
Pearson Family Butcher
Ashton-under-Lyne market hall

Sillfields Farm, Cumbria
(wild boar, black pudding,
all sorts of meat)
www.sillfield.co.uk

Deana and Allan Parkinson,
butchers in Greater Eccleston

Turnbulls Butchers, Alnwick
www.turnbullsofalnwick.co.uk

Fruit and vegetables

Yorkshire asparagus
www.british-asparagus.co.uk/
blog/?tag=ronda-morritt

Barton and Redman,
Manchester
www.bartonandredman.com

Ampleforth Orchards
http://www.abbey.ampleforth.org.
uk/our-work/orchards/

Yorkshire forced rhubarb
www.yorkshirerhubarb.co.uk

Sauces

Henderson's relish
www.hendersonsrelish.com

For sauces, jams and all kinds of Yorkshire foods

www.theyorkshirepantry.com

Baking

Skidby Mill (Council run!)
in the Yorkshire Wolds is
the only remaining wind-
powered (four-sailed tower)
flour mill in Yorkshire. The
flour they produce is a strong
wholemeal – fabulous for
bread
http://www2.eastriding.gov.uk/
leisure/museums-and-galleries/
east-riding-museums-and-
galleries/skidby-mill

Puddings

Cartmel Village Shop
www.cartmelvillageshop.co.uk

Drinks

Oliver Haussels,
C & O Wines
www.cowines.com

Richardson's wine shop
in Whitehaven
www.richardsonsofwhitehaven.
co.uk

Timothy Taylor's Landlords
Ale, Keighley
www.timothytaylor.co.uk

Other breweries worth a
visit are Newcastle Brown,
Tadcaster; Hawkshead
Brewery and Jennings
Brewery, Cumbria; the
Millstone Brewery, The
Greenfield Brewery and
the Marble Arch Brewery,
Manchester

INDEX

ACKNOWLEDGEMENTS

I'd like to give a great big thanks to all the chefs who have become pals over the years, including Simon Hopkinson, Paul Heathcote, Shaun Hill and Jean-Christophe Novelli. I've used recipes by Simon, Paul and Shaun in this book. Thanks also to Bob Kitching for introducing me to cheesemaking, and to Lindsay Bareham and Grub Street Publishers for letting us use her ketchup recipe.

On a personal note, thanks to Tony Veg at New Smithfields Market, Gerard Richardson and family of Cumbria, and songwriter Ian McNabb.

On the publishing side, thanks to Fiona Henderson for typing up all the recipes for us, Gill Paul for helping to put together the text for this book, Kay Halsey the meticulous copyeditor, and our editor Sarah Hammond and all the team at Hodder.

A big thanks to Geoff Lloyd our location photographer, Amanda Heywood our food photographer, Polly Webb-Wilson the book's food stylist, and Ash Western our designer. Your talent has made this book very special.

On the TV side; Jazz Gowans, Richard Hughes, Mark Powell, Kerry Allison, Sean McGuiness, Lee Suttersby, James Arnold, Merryn Threadgould, Norah Quartey, Simon Coran, and the star that is Blair Yates, as well as all the incredible contributors we met on our Northern travels.

Thanks also to my agent Teresa Quinlan and Debby Lee of Argonon.

Huge thanks to Elsie Kerr from Newcastle for her magnificent pie recipe, to Bette Paul from Glasgow for her steamed pudding, to Mrs Maureen Gowans from Crewe for her recipe suggestions and finally to Mogs Hughes for her tips on the best brown bread ice cream north or south of Manchester.

Thanks to Anne Connolly at Larkton Hall Farm for her tips on Alpine cheese. Cheesy leeks made with Crabtree never tasted so good.

Thanks to Mandy Wragg, Northern food consultant, for her advice on this book. See her great website www.squidbeak.co.uk for recommendations on where to eat in the North.

Thanks to Giles Bennett, the finest source of Yorkshire food at www.theyorkshirepantry.com

Matt Sefton, the cocktail shaker man – you're a star!

Finally, Rev and I would like to thank our respective families and friends for the ever-present support and encouragement over the years.

Rock on!